D0482944

James Friesen

About the Author

Victor Carl Friesen was born and raised on the family farm near Rosthern, Saskatchewan, during the Great Depression. His passion for history was awakened at an early age as the depression dust storms uncovered arrowheads on his family's land.

A natural teacher, Friesen taught in a variety of settings over the years—rural one-room school, town school, university, technical institute, and community college—while pursuing his interests in history, natural history, literature, singing, painting, and photography on the side. In 1983, he left teaching to become a full-time freelance writer.

Friesen has penned five books: *The Spirit of Huckleberry*, *The Mulberry Tree*, *The Windmill Turning*, *The Year is a Circle*, and *Where the River Runs*. His more than 200 essays, articles, fiction, and poetry have appeared in numerous magazines, journals, and anthologies.

Friesen now lives in his hometown of Rosthern, Saskatchewan, with his wife Dorothy; thus, he can and does return to his boyhood farm as often as possible to putter around the place that is forever home.

TO MERRILEE DAVEY

Forever Home
A good old days on the farm

VICTOR CARL FRIESEN

FIFTH
HOUSE

Cover and interior design by Kathy Aldous-Schleindl
Cover and interior illustrations by Cheryl Peddie
Edited by Geri Rowlatt
Copyedited by Meaghan Craven
Proofread by Ann Sullivan
Scans by St. Solo Computer Graphics

The publisher gratefully acknowledges the support of The Canada Council for the Arts and the Department of Canadian Heritage.

THE CANADA COUNCIL | LE CONSEIL DES ARTS
FOR THE ARTS | DU CANADA
SINCE 1957 | DEPUIS 1957

We acknowledge the financial support of the Government of Canada through the Book Publishing Industry Development Program (BPIDP) for our publishing activities.

Printed in Canada by Friesens

04 05 06 07 08 / 5 4 3 2 1

First published in the United States in 2005 by
Fitzhenry & Whiteside
121 Harvard Avenue, Suite 2
Allston, MA 02134

National Library of Canada Cataloguing in Publication
Friesen, Victor Carl
    Forever home : good old days on the farm / Victor Carl Friesen.

ISBN 1-894856-42-2
1. Friesen, Victor Carl–Childhood and youth. 2. Friesen, Victor Carl–Family.
3. Farm life–Saskatchewan–Rosthern Region–Anecdotes.
4. Rosthern Region (Sask.)–Social life and customs–20th century.
5. Rosthern Region (Sask.)–Biography. I. Title.

FC3549.R67Z49 2004   971.24'202'092   C2004-902905-3

Fifth House Ltd.
A Fitzhenry & Whiteside Company
1511, 1800-4 St. SW
Calgary, Alberta T2S 2S5
1-800-387-9776
www.fitzhenry.ca

Contents

Foreword

Several times a week I walk past a large, multi-storied building called "The Heritage." The title cuts a little too near the bone, for this high-rise shelters the aging refugees of the subsistence farm culture that truly is our heritage. In a civilization that has reduced rural life to caricatures of the unsophisticated rube and the inbred redneck, such glib homage rankles. A seniors' complex like this one is full of people who, for one reason or another, left the farm life of their upbringing. Now, as they close out their years in the city, they sit in the quiet of their rooms and remember. At some distance from meadowlark song and lamplight, they recall, nonetheless, the music their mother played in the living room, the smell of scalded hens, and the sight of children skating on ponds. Few of them have the capacity to write it down as beautifully as Vic Friesen has in this memoir, but their memories are just as vivid and present in their minds.

Good memoir requires at least two things: one, a voice that is authentic, engaging, and worthy of the reader's trust, and, two, a narrative that binds the personal to the universal. The book you have in your hands meets the first requirement easily because Vic Friesen is Vic Friesen—someone who grew up on a homestead where literature and imagination equipped him to become a storyteller and an articulate observer of lifeways that are now gone. Satisfying the second requirement—to project memory against the wider horizon of human experience—Friesen speaks with affection and great respect, not only to the generation that remembers along with him, but also to the generations subsequent, which now must strain to imagine what that life-investing labor in field and kitchen might have been like.

The narrative takes the reader season by season through what Wendell Berry has called the "customs of necessity." These are the everyday, callus-forming tasks of securing food and shelter that, rather than mere drudgery, become transforming rituals that sear themselves into the memory and protect the personal bond to place. In lovingly observed descriptions of days on a Rosthern area farm in the 1930s and '40s, Friesen gives us the view from the hayloft, his mother's simple pancake recipe, butter down the well, and so much more. Drawn into his confidence, we see the trail that leads from town, the school rink flooded bucket by bucket, the cream pouring out of the separator, the ham in the smoke house—and as image after image accumulates in the mind, the inevitable question comes: where are we now that this innocence has fled, now that men seed tracts of land fifty times the size of the Friesen farm, now that toxic levels of pesticides are collecting in breast milk? Friesen leaves that for us to answer, but any honest response we might offer is shot through with regret and compromised by modern comforts we are disinclined to forgo.

The temptation, of course, is always to cling to the past, even wish for its return, but, as Friesen knows too well, there is no going back. As prairie people, we are living in a time of cultural transition when, as difficult as it may seem, letting go is the only way to receive the blessings of our heritage. In the end, that is what writers like Vic Friesen do for us when they put their memories down on paper. These stories pass on benedictions borne in lifeways seeded and husbanded by our ancestors. As long as we keep reseeding them in narratives, the blessings remain for others to take up should we ever have need or desire to stir to life something of their spirit within the soil of here and now on these plains.

Trevor Herriot
Author of *River in a Dry Land*

Preface

I was born on a sandy, quarter-section farm (160 acres) near Rosthern, Saskatchewan, in 1933. The farm had been part of an unused school section and so was still virgin land when my father bought it with a dollar down payment eighteen years earlier. (This was during the First World War, a time of high prices.) Married with a growing family, he and Mother worked contentedly to pay off the mortgage, but with the Great Depression intervening, it was 1944 before the land was finally ours. Imagine—twenty-nine years to pay off a $4,000 farmstead! Of course, by then the mortgage had become more than double that amount because of interest charges. Such is the setting for *Forever Home: Good Old Days on the Farm.*

Only a hundred acres were cultivated and only three-fourths of that number were planted in any one spring. Crops were cut with a binder throughout the 1940s, stooked by hand, and threshed with an old-time separator. The rest of the sandy (and alkaline) soil was left as pasture or meadowland with a scattering of poplar bushes and wolf willow. It was a terrain best suited for mixed farming. And so we had a few cows, some pigs, and a flock of chickens to tend. My daily job was to water the cows (and two horses) at a bucket-and-pulley well a quarter-mile from the yard— wells, hand dug in those days, went dry closer to home. Other activities included fishing at the South Saskatchewan River, six miles away, and scrounging the pasture bushes for dry trees in fall, to be sawn up into a huge woodpile for our winter's fuel.

Winters in the 1940s, it seemed, always had prodigious amounts of snow, and my personal means of getting around—to the district's rural school, for instance—was a pair of homemade skis. Skiing cross-country, I traveled in a boy's private imaginary world of northern plains and bitter cold. From January through March during grades nine and ten, which I took by correspondence courses, I did my schoolwork at our dining-room table. So, too, I took my entire grade eleven, without having my lessons corrected—it was cheaper that way—and then writing my final examinations in town in June. In this manner I stayed close to our farm and the surrounding outdoor world throughout my youth.

It has been said that you can take a boy out of the farm but you cannot take the farm out of the boy. I both left and stayed after my father died in 1950. Mother still lived there, without electricity, during the summers into the 1970s—to her it was the best place to be—and by then I had bought the farm where I was born. She died in 1988.

The youngest child in the family, I am now the only one left. We all shared our parents' affection for olden-day farm life. A rural-school teacher before she married, my sister, with her husband, bought the quarter section touching corners with the "home place" and farmed it on weekends. My older brother, although a Royal Canadian Mounted Policeman stationed in British Columbia and Ontario, returned for his holidays every fall to savor harvest time on the prairies. In fact, he and I jointly owned the farm for several years, and he and his wife retired to Rosthern to keep in closer touch. My other brother worked in town for the local rural municipality, staying abreast of farm activities, and when he later moved to the city, he and his wife tried to come out every weekend in summer just to see "how things were."

As for me, I left teaching (eventually at university and community college) to take up freelance writing full time in 1983 at Rosthern. Although my work prevents me from living on a non-electrified farm, I return to it as often as possible—mowing the yard, pruning the trees, walking nostalgically to the hay meadow, hearing geese overhead, sensing the great night coming on, and recalling my parents' dedication to this one plot of land that is forever home.

Henry David Thoreau says that nature is "one and continuous everywhere." That also describes rural life in those simpler times sixty years ago: back then it was much the same in small farms across our country and the bordering United States. In writing this book, I have told the story of my own 1940s boyhood, trying to capture the sights and sounds of memorable experiences. The chapters, grouped into sections of related activities, can be read independently. My gratitude goes to my wife, Dorothy, for her special care in reading the original manuscript and for offering suggestions from a city girl's perspective.

I

INTRODUCTIONS

Family Portrait

My mother had her first picture taken on going home from her pioneer school near Rosthern, Saskatchewan. Nine years old and in grade three, she was walking with her sister, another schoolgirl from a neighboring farm, and their new teacher, who boarded at that farm. Along the way a young man from town came by unexpectedly in his shiny black buggy and offered them a ride. When they reached the saline lake on my mother's farm, with the autumn glory of its surrounding trees reflected there, he stopped the buggy and said, "It should make a nice picture." He had a camera with him; the film, of course, was black and white.

The young women dismounted and gazed self-consciously at their photographer. Mother and her sister were wearing new dresses (not a regular school practice then), which their oldest sister had made for them. The material was a practical gray, hard-textured cloth (sure to be long-wearing), but the under-

1

standing sister had adorned the skirts with two black bands and had made black tams to match. It was a proud moment for Mother to stand beside her teacher and have her picture snapped.

Photographs remained special to Mother, particularly as they recorded highlights of her own growing family's history. She insisted that a professional wedding portrait be taken of her and Dad, even though, in 1918, their quarter-section farm was entirely in debt, their house was an uninsulated fourteen-by-twenty-foot shack, and living was but a daily scrounging to make do.

Thus, a week after their wedding, they donned their wedding garb once more—Mother in a homemade dress, this time of her own making—and rode to the photographer's studio in town. (Formal wedding-day photos of farm couples were rare because their weddings usually occurred in a cleaned-out granary, the only adequate spacious facility available.)

In the portrait Mother looks firmly ahead, as into the future, committed yet not quite knowing what to expect, her hand secure in the crook of Dad's arm. Dad smiles slightly, stalwart and pleased. Just turned thirty-four since the marriage, he is fifteen years older than Mother (their birthdays are on the same day).

After the first two children were born, another studio portrait was taken. It was now the mid-1920s. Mother stands stoically in the center with her family before her. Dad sits comfortably in an armchair to one side, Mother's hand resting on the back. My sister, Elsie, looking apprehensive and strong-willed at the same time, sits on a cushioned small tabletop on the other side, with Mother's other arm supporting her. The younger Ernie sits in a folding chair in front of her, with an arm on Dad's knee. His expression, even for one so young, suggests, if anything, disbelief.

The 1930s were drawing to a close before the next family portrait was considered. By then the Great Depression—a market crash and the severest drought on record—had swept over the prairies for a full decade. Our farm was even more in debt because of accumulated interest, and 1937 had marked an utter crop failure, with not enough standing grain to warrant cutting.

Yet in the spring of 1939, Mother felt it was the last chance for a formal photograph of her family before the oldest children started leaving home. Elsie was nineteen, Ernie seventeen, and either might get work as hired help somewhere. The chances of Elsie or Ernie completing grade twelve seemed slim. (They, in fact, did finish high school after a hiatus of a few years from education.)

There were also only four children now—Elsie, Ernie, Ted, aged thirteen, and me, a preschool five. Two others had died and would never be in a family portrait—Rosie, succumbing to whooping cough at just a year, next in line to Ernie; and Richard, dying at birth, who would have filled the gap between Ted and me. Even Ted had had rheumatic fever, which affected his heart and severely restricted his physical activities.

So Mother made an appointment for a sitting with "John Mahler's Photo" in town. I do not remember what the fee was (or whether it was paid in cash or produce), but a date was circled on the calendar for the photograph session.

For some reason our parents chose not to be in the photograph. Perhaps the fee was too high if adults were included. Perhaps they felt their appearance was just too Depression-worn to be forever remembered through the mere clicking of a camera. Their concern was for us to look our best and then get us to the studio.

The project was not undertaken lightly. First, we all had to have something decent to wear. Elsie's white voile dress and red silk sash were fashioned by Mother on a treadle sewing machine. To complete the outfit, my sister wore matching white sandals.

Actually, the sewing machine did quadruple duty. After sewing white shirts for Ted and me, and my trousers as well, Mother used it to take in an old suit coat to fit Ernie. His pants did not matter since, as the tallest in the family, he would be posed behind the rest of us children. His striped blue tie and freshly ironed shirt were what would be noticed.

Ted and I each had ties too, found somewhere in the back of our parents' chiffonier. Ted's was one of those permanently tied neckpieces, striped and somewhat too short for him. An elastic band fastened it around his neck. Mine was also held snug with an elastic band but was a bow tie for which there was hardly room under my chin.

The only newly bought item of clothing was Ted's black denim pants. They would look close enough to real dress slacks in a black and white photo and could be worn as everyday apparel after that. However, the waist closed with a telltale nickeled snap fastener and would slip revealingly below his belt in one of the photos.

Now, on the day of our appointment, we had only to clean up, look to our hair, and take the slow dusty wagon trip to town. My hair was the easiest to manage. As a preschooler, I wore it in dark brown bangs across my forehead. So Mother clipped them—she cut the hair in our family (and, without charge, that of several neighbors as well).

Ted, dark like me, combed his hair to the side, while Ernie wore his straight back. Elsie's fell becomingly in soft waves, a pair of curling tongs heated over the coal-oil lamp chimney used to achieve the proper effect. (She and Ernie were fair, taking after Dad.)

There was only one last consideration. The long, hot trip into town would be hard on our fine clothes, particularly Elsie's voile dress. Mother checked beforehand to be sure that my sister could change at the studio, which was but a spare room at the photographer's house. We were ready for the auspicious day.

Just two photographs were taken that afternoon. In the first, we are standing—Elsie and Ted together, Ernie centered behind, and I in front. Ernie stood on a small stool, which remained hidden from view (as did his trousers). We look pleasant enough: Elsie, already a young woman anticipating the future; Ernie, a somewhat lanky and pale older teenager having shot up in height recently; Ted, a bright new teenager caught up in the day's venture; and I, a dutiful small boy trying not to move.

We are all looking directly into the camera, a box-like bellows affair holding slide-in negative plates and draped with a black cloth, the photographer having disappeared beneath it to snap the picture. I was fascinated with the whole procedure and watched the man's every move.

The second photograph was the better one, taken closer up. We are all sitting—Elsie, Ted, and I in a row, hands resting lightly in our laps, and Ernie behind, looking out between Elsie and Ted. Thus we are in chronological order, oldest to youngest, left to right. And the faces of the three of us in front are in a descending diagonal.

We ordered a few reproductions of each photograph, four by five-and-a-half-inch prints. Some were sent away to close friends and relatives, and some were kept to show proudly to any visitors who dropped by. On the copy I am looking at today—recently returned to me by a distant relative—Mother had written: "Best wishes from the Abe Friesen family."

Yes, there we were for all to see: Elsie, Ernie, Ted, and Vic. Mother, in showing the two pictures to her guests (Dad was content to sit and let her "explain" the photos), always named each of us. Mother's pride in a studio photograph of her children was only complete if our names were mentioned, names carefully chosen at our birth. Elsie had but one Christian name, from the *Elsie Dinsmore* books that Mother had once read, but my sister herself took on the second name of Anne (spelled with an "e") from the *Anne of Green Gables* books that *she* read. Ernie was named for Ernest in *Swiss Family Robinson*, another of Mother's childhood reading adventures, and bore Dad's name of Abram as well. Ted was named for a president and a prime minister—Theodore Roosevelt and Wilfrid Laurier—and most pleased to be so honored.

Originally I was to have been Leo Victor, but when Dad went to town to register me, the official was away. Mother was pleased at this turn of events, for she had started to regret the name Leo (really, her oldest sister's suggestion). So a new name was chosen, and she insisted that Dad for once should do the choosing. Well, Dad thought *Carl* was a stalwart-sounding name, and I became Victor Carl, a name I have prized over the years—for its euphony, I think—and, as a writer, have always used in full.

As we grew up and eventually left home, there were more formal photographs taken of Elsie Anne, Ernest Abram, Theodore Wilfrid, and Victor Carl, individually. Elsie had a tinted photo made of herself at a Saskatoon photographer's studio, later sending a reproduction of it to her fiancé serving overseas in the Second World War. Ernie had a photo taken of himself as an RCMP officer, Ted as a newlywed with his wife, and I as a university graduate.

All of these were mounted, and Mother, now a widow, displayed them atop her pedal organ and again showed them to her guests, naming each of us in turn. But I believe these four new photos did not carry with them quite the same thrill, for her or for us, as the two small prints of us children together, taken in the Depression years. That was a whole little adventure in itself that always bore another warm nostalgic "explaining," even amongst ourselves whenever we got together.

In the 1960s Mother had a formal color photo taken of herself: a keepsake for each of her children. She wore, as adornments, gifts from two family members already gone—a pearl necklace, a wedding present from Dad, who died in 1950; and single-pearl earrings from Ted, who died as a young man of twenty-eight, a consequence of childhood rheumatic fever. (She was so afraid of losing these that she screwed them extra tight, and the earlobe showing on the picture is slightly red.)

Mother, at last wearing a store-bought dress, now white-haired and wearing glasses, is smiling confidently, her expressive brown eyes full of love and understanding. In this photo of her I can also see the nine-year-old girl standing proudly beside her teacher, having her first picture taken. I can see, too, the inner security that is revealed in her wedding photo—her hand crooked safely onto Dad's arm—in the assurance of Dad's pearls about her neck. She looks with the same expectancy into the years ahead. And as in the family photo of her and Dad and the two small children, her face exhibits a similar strength and resolve.

The present photo shows someone who has wonderfully survived the Great Depression, someone who has fought the battle of a full life and won. If photographs were special to Mother in highlighting her own family's growth, this photo of her, taken in her senior years, was special to her children.

She was our keeper of the hearth, the maker of the home in which we all were born, in which all our growing lives were centered and nurtured. Just seeing the picture, I sense once more the determination and sacrifice exhibited by her, and by Dad, in having our own very special 1939 portrait taken.

The House that Grow'd

On my desk is a black and white picture of the house in which I
was born. It is a little gray shack, fourteen by twenty feet in size,
standing a lone sentinel on the Saskatchewan parklands.

In front of the house, on the porch step, sit my small brother
and sister, barefoot, wearing homemade coveralls and straw hats.
My sister's hat has a wide ribbon around the crown. Leaning
against the front wall are two lumpy sacks of potatoes. A chicken
stands nearby and, with head turned sideways, eyes the photographer, my mother with her Kodak Junior bellows camera.

It is not a prosperous scene despite the two full potato sacks.
The house has no foundation, the three windows have neither
screens nor storm windows, and the door is made only of boards.
It could well have been the model for that olden-day song, "Little Grey Home in the West."

One feature bespeaks possible better times and seems
entirely incongruous on the little shack—a set of three lightning

arresters pointing up into the sky from the slanting roof. While the picture cannot show their full "grandeur," each arrester has an octagonal glass globe of bright blue. I don't know if lightning strikes were more common or powerful in the early days, but, apparently, lightning-arrester salesmen were. Many of the old farmhouses that I remember from my boyhood were graced by such safety devices.

My siblings and I were all born in this little house, and it is with a kind of inverse snobbery that I direct visitors' attention to the picture. Actually, when my "snobbery" has not got the best of me, I admit that by the time I came along, the shack had had an addition built onto it. Still, I am glad I was born in the shack.

In olden times it was customary for houses to have "grow'd" like Topsy in *Uncle Tom's Cabin*. A pioneer would start with a small dwelling and then add lean-tos or other structures as the family increased. Our house was originally built in 1917, with further additions in each of the next three decades.

Really, my father had haphazardly constructed the shack as a temporary home during the First World War. Good lumber was hard to come by then, and he had used splintery boards with no insulation between the outer and inner walls. With his first full crop completely hailed out and the land bought on time, there was no hope of improving the house. He married the next year, and my parents lived for the next eight years in this provisional home.

By then three children had been born. In wintertime, my mother told me, the frost on the windows was an inch thick, that is, level with the wooden frame—because of the diaper washing done inside. Dad, meanwhile, would shovel snow against the outside walls, as high as the windowsills, for insulation.

When Ted was born in 1926, something had to be done to create more living space. Money was borrowed, and a pitched-roof addition—with insulation and even plasterboard—was built endwise against the front of the shack. It began as a single room, later had a bedroom walled off at one end, then reverted to a living/dining room.

The addition had one failing. It formed a right angle with the shack, opening on the southwest, and the hot afternoon summer sun was simply scorching in that corner. Since the house's entrance was located there, there was no way of even beginning to keep the house cool. So in 1933, the year of my birth, a little porch was built on.

When I was a youngster, the shack was partitioned into a kitchen and a boys' bedroom. Every winter, lines of rime appeared along the boards on the inside north wall, despite the snow banked on the other side. I slept next to the wall and soon learned not to roll over in bed too quickly in my sleep, tugging my quilt with me. The quilt could easily freeze to the wall, and nobody liked a torn quilt-cover.

The final spurt in the development of the house that "grow'd" occurred in 1943. That year the little porch/lean-to was extended to run the length of the earlier pitched-roof addition, providing one more room. The house could now boast a kitchen, living/dining room, two bedrooms, and a porch. It had taken thirty-six years to reach full growth.

During that time the house had rarely been painted, but not through my mother's choice. She had heard somewhere a paint slogan, "Save the surface and you save all." In 1918 she wanted to do her best to brighten up the little shack, her first home of married life, and immediately got Dad to buy some paint. This she brushed on energetically but soon found that it dried in wrinkles. We learned later that some paint made during the First World War (with its shortages) had a fish-oil base and was not of good quality.

Then came hard times, and then really hard times during the Great Depression, and the little home in the west got grayer and grayer. Whenever Mother and Dad rounded the last bend in the trail coming home from town in the Bennett wagon, Mother would close her eyes. That drab structure was not the house she wanted to see.

In the 1940s times were better, but we were now in another

world war with further shortages. Mother and Dad first tried whitewash. Unfortunately, things did not go right, and after a few rains the white coloring washed off and covered the ground next to the walls and not the house.

With their distrust of wartime paints, they next decided to mix their own. A mixture of raw linseed oil and white lead proved reliable. From then on we had a "White House," brilliant in the sunshine, with dark green trim. This was no eyesore to be glimpsed from a distance.

So the house remained, without change. Although finances improved, there was never enough money to wire the house for electricity, despite a rural electrification program. Nor was plumbing installed. When my father died, Mother moved to Saskatoon and took up day-work each winter but returned to live in her little house on the prairie for six months every summer. (She continued doing so for a few years, even two decades later after retiring to Rosthern.)

Her relatives advised her against returning, but not to return? She never even considered it. Mother enjoyed doing the simple necessary tasks about the house, such as carrying in well water or lighting the coal-oil lamps at evening. Meanwhile, a crackling fire in the stove took away the evening's chill, and the kettle, freshly filled, steamed away.

When my holidays came round each summer, I, too, headed home, like a salmon to its natal stream. For me, to saw and split wood for the fires and see to the upkeep of the house was a rejuvenation of the spirit.

The years slipped by, Mother growing old with the house, the home that became ever dearer to her (and to me). The house had her affection just as a close family member might. "Hello, little house," she greeted it in spring, and "Goodbye, little house" were her parting words in fall.

Finally, increasing age made her being there alone impractical. Yet for her, in spite of all the modern conveniences and the activities and companionship of life in town, the little prairie house was "still the best place to be." These would always be her words on leaving, even when she could go for only an afternoon's stay.

Although my association with the house, my birthplace, was so much shorter than my mother's, I knew something of what she felt. The house had grown and changed over the decades, even as we had. We had molded it to our needs, and it, in its way, had molded us. It represented a part of us and would continue to be inseparable from our lives.

The Kitchen Table

The most important piece of furniture in our farmhouse was the kitchen table. We gathered around it three times each day for our meals and then set out, nourished and renewed, to our varied activities. It was a starting point and a destination: the center of our family communication network, a workplace, and safe haven all in one.

To accommodate our family of six, Dad made a narrow bench to seat two children along one side (it fit between the table legs and wall when the table was pushed out of the way after meals). The others sat on spindle-backed chairs, Dad at one end and Mother, nearest the kitchen range, next to him on the adjacent side.

As youngest, I sat on a separate tiny bench set upon the narrow one—not as precarious as it seems. I had the wall (and the window) immediately behind me, the table in front, my older brother on my right, and Dad, with his capable reach, to my left. "More potatoes, please!"

The kitchen table, of course, was used to prepare food as much as to present it. The table stood to one side between the kitchen cabinet, with its work counter, and the cooking range. Thus food might have its origin at the cabinet and its nearby flour bin—the mixing of dough, for instance—but the final product—bread, buns, or cookies—would be made on the table.

A fascination of childhood was to sit beside the table while Mother flattened a huge lump of dough with her hands or rolled it out with wooden rolling pin, then to see her cut or shape it into smaller objects for baking. Biscuits pressed out with the edge of a glass tumbler or cut into diamonds with a few deft knife strokes; buns rolled out as if by sleight of hand from ragged gobs, two at a time, one hand moving clockwise, the other counter-clockwise; loaves produced magically, like sudden white mushrooms, their bottoms crimped tight, and placed in a baking pan: these were the feats of legerdemain practiced every few days on the homely kitchen table.

Equally fascinating were the preparations made for that favorite of meals, roast chicken. The chicken did not come from the supermarket. It patrolled the henyard outside, and so this bill of fare first came to the kitchen table via the chopping block at the woodpile. Then it had to be plucked (with the help of boiling water to loosen the feathers), singed (over some burning crumpled newspaper atop the range), and eviscerated.

This last operation held our particular attention, and the removal of the gizzard was of chief interest. Of bluish-green color with a white pearly luster, it was shaped like a shuffleboard disk. Mother cut out two notches on opposite sides, slit through the top, and peeled the whole thing apart into a trim giblet, vied for at mealtime as a special treat.

A few times a week the kitchen table was reserved for Dad for a very formal occasion—shaving with a straight razor. We children sat alongside, watching the action. (Like most farm homes then, ours did not have running water, and the washstand was built too low for adults—so children might use it more easily.)

Dad made the most of the activity, what with a rapt audience before him. He stropped the blade with a flourish, lathered his face abundantly from a neat china shaving bowl (our granite wash basin stood handy on the stove with hot water), and puck-ered his face in readiness before the portable mirror on the table. Then with the razor opened more than 180 degrees from its horn handle, he tentatively scraped a bit of foam from one side of his face. Everything well and good, he proceeded across his face in a definite pattern, pulling the skin taut to facilitate a close shave, grimacing with his mouth to shave carefully about the lips, finally finishing, or so it seemed to us, with abandon as he swung the blade upward in a series of fast sweeps under the chin. Never once did he cut himself. All done, with a knowing look at us, and rubbing his smooth skin, he cleaned up his gear and put it away till the next time. End of show.

So many other activities occurred at the kitchen table. Mother ironed clothes on it (preferring its breadth to that of the narrow ironing board) and laid out patterns there when cutting fabric for new clothes. Dad used it for minor carpentry jobs and home repairs during the winter when the shop outdoors was too cold. We children played on it, devising castles from stacks of old books or using its smooth oilcloth cover for the ice surface of a miniature hockey game.

It was also a place for rest and counsel. When Dad needed a break from his outdoor labors, he came inside to relax in his usual kitchen chair, pulled out sideways to let him stretch out his legs toward the warm stove and rest one elbow on the table. Mother, glad to be off her feet from her running-around-all-day household chores, would join him for coffee, still too hot to drink, and consider their day's work thus far. As they conversed, we children sometimes gravitated there, too, somehow feeling we were part of the adult world of cares and responsibilities.

Important family decisions were usually made about the kitchen table. One of those, I remember, affected me directly. I had no skates at the time, and the children at our rural school had made an outdoor skating rink. One of them had offered to sell me his second-hand skates for $2.50. That was a lot of money to our family then, and we had to discuss the weighty affair—naturally around our kitchen table.

My older brothers and sister argued that they had not had skates at my age—I was all of nine—and I would soon outgrow them. What use would they be then? I countered that they were good quality "tube" skates and would have resale value. My parents thought that if my fellow students had skates, I should have a pair, too. They would find the money. After I solemnly vowed to take good care of them, they "outvoted" my siblings, much to my glee.

The following supper was a time of quiet elation for me, but really not that different from most end-of-day meals about our kitchen table. A day's work had been accomplished—and that well done to earn a night's repose. There was a feeling of closeness, of experiences shared, and of harmony and security. The coal-oil lamp, freshly lit, cast a warm glow on the food spread appetizingly before us—and on each of us as well. Heads bowed in silent prayer, we were about the kitchen table again, feeling an inner strength and bliss in family togetherness. Always the kitchen table, always fine memories to remain with us. The poet Edna Jaques writes in "Inner Life" (from *My Kitchen Window*, John H. Hopkins & Son, 1936):

The fire when laid … the supper-table spread,
Even the simple breaking of the bread,
Are symbols of diviner things that lie
Close to our inner selves and will not die.

The Cellar

The cellar was a special place. Not only was it an underground storage for all the good things grown in our garden each summer but also a unique spot to play, as fabulous as Robinson Crusoe's cavern, with a little imagination. It was quite small, underlying just part of the kitchen.

Some years Mother canned more than a hundred quarts of fruits and vegetables, and they lined the cellar shelves in appetizing display. Peas, like green pearls, filled a dozen or so jars, while adjacent sealers held long yellow beans. Dark wine pickled beets and golden-shelled corn added further color, as did the red and green rhubarb. Wild fruits were used in various preserves—highbush-cranberry jam (my favorite), chokecherries as a thin spread for pancakes or as an ingredient for *mooss* (a side dish with a thickening of flour), and finally saskatoon compote or jam. Peaches, apricots, pears, and crabapples—bought in season—also were canned and stored on the shelves.

It was a treat to go down in the cellar to select a jar as dessert for that evening's meal. One could choose for color or taste and never be disappointed. All had the coolness imparted by storage in the earth and the savor of ripe autumn days. The many odors associated with the cellar made a trip down the steps a notable experience. Combined with the expected earthy smell, there were odors from potatoes drying in their bin and turnips suspended from floor joists and from the huge ten-gallon crock where fermenting cabbage was becoming tasty sauerkraut.

There might be a pickling crock, too, of cucumbers and pungent dill and translucent onions. In early winter, after pig butchering, another crock, filled with brine or whey, would hold pickled pig's feet and headcheese. One could descend with a bowl to spear a few dills with a fork or slice some headcheese for dinner or supper. The flavorful contents of these crocks gave zest to any meal.

The jars of preserves, meanwhile, could remain in attractive rows, without causing clutter, right through one winter season and into the next if need be. Only turnips and carrots not covered with sand had to be eaten before they withered away, while the potatoes persisted in sprouting.

Some time in mid-winter and again in spring, someone, usually Mother, would go into the cellar with a lighted lantern, hang it on an overhead nail, and begin the tedious task of "de-sprouting" the potatoes. Sitting on an overturned pail beside the bin, she would rip the long white shoots off each potato, then place the potato on a separate pile, the sprouts to one side. The job could go on for hours and yield bucketfuls of sprouts for the cows to munch on. They liked something fresh and juicy as a change from the usual dry hay.

I remember one time when Mother—who had already made three meals that day, helped with the milking morning and evening, washed out the cream separator (and washed and dried the dishes from each meal), and churned five gallons of cream into butter—started to work on the sprouting potatoes before the day was out. "Mother," my older brother, Ernie, called down into the cellar, "if I had as much energy as you, I'd be a millionaire."

Perhaps she just wanted a chance to sit down and rest her feet or perhaps she found the cool cellar a nice quiet place to be. Maybe she was thinking of the delights she had had as a little girl playing in the cellar at her own parents' home.

Certainly we children found amusement in our cellar. The

weekly *Free Press Prairie Farmer* at the time carried the funny paper "King of the Royal Mounted," one installment of which pictured the hero deep-sea diving in an investigation of stolen treasure. It was before scuba techniques, and King plunged into the depths wearing heavy gear and a diving helmet. My cousin and I immediately made our own helmets and descended one step at a time, past the raised trapdoor and into the murky depths to explore for "treasure" there.

Our diving helmets were of two kinds. One was a corrugated cardboard box with peepholes cut on three sides. The other required more imagination, for it was constructed of Tinkertoy. Still, it served our purpose admirably and, like the real thing, needed to be unlatched (pulled apart at the collar) before the wearer, on coming up, could relate his "underwater" adventure.

The only amphibious creatures we saw below were the salamanders that liked to tunnel in the earthen walls. But occasionally there were other animals, and these, unlike the innocuous salamanders, could be real pests. Mice were a problem, no matter how "wee, sleekit, cowrin, tim'rous" they seemed to be, peering out with gleaming eye from between two jars of peaches in the light of an upheld lantern. Traps had to be set for them. And sometimes gophers dug burrows under the kitchen's stone foundation, near the little cellar. They seldom ventured into the cellar itself, but their digging might have allowed badgers or skunks to finally gain entrance.

Skunks were the worst possible nuisance. A discharge of their scent spray, when the animals were suddenly surprised, could make a cellar unusable for an entire summer. One year we had a nest of young skunks under the floor joists adjacent to the cellar, and it was only with extreme care that we eventually got rid of them.

Alan Devoe, the naturalist, writes in *This Fascinating Animal World* (McGraw-Hill, 1951) that skunk smell can well be formidable, but that just a faint whiff of it is an "earth-evocative thing," an awakening of "fresh responsiveness to the old excitement of

19

the earth." This excitement, he says, fades away as we grow out of childhood, but can be aroused again by a minute drift of this primitive earthy odor.

Perhaps the attraction of a cellar to a child (and to an adult looking nostalgically back at childhood) was its overall earthiness—in smell and feel and sight. It spoke to something primeval in us, perhaps stirring something in our memory about dim, damp caves used as larders and shelters in earliest times.

So we reminisce about cellars, thankful we could experience them as children, feeling the earthen floor with our bare feet, smelling the musty odors of the damp walls, and seeing the stored preserves and garden produce. It is somehow satisfying that although a deserted farmhouse may be in ruins or have been moved away, the old cellar remains, that treasured place of long ago, outlasting its more sophisticated superstructure.

Our Old Smokehouse

Only one log building remains standing in our farmyard—the smokehouse. It served our family for many years. A five-by-six-foot structure, eight feet high at the peak, it shows little sign of decay, the smoke-darkened logs as sturdy as ever. But the mud-and-straw plaster that once coated the outer walls has fallen off, and the shingled roof is covered with moss. It has not been used since 1950, when my father died.

The building is of special interest to me, for it was built the year I was born. It was constructed with care: the logs, fifteen on a side up to the eaves, were notched on the underside only, so that rain would run off and not soak into the wood. The doorway is purposely small—barely wide enough to squeeze through in an otherwise stout wall—and its two-and-a-half-foot opening begins three logs up from the ground. The door, of fine-grained boards, is fastened with rusty hinges and closes with a swivel.

Inside are two short joists, seven feet high, with five spikes nailed into each of them. From these the curing meat would hang, and a half-dozen wire meathooks still are looped over a nail on an inside wall. A small wooden chimney, extending through the peak, now serves as a little "skylight." When the sun is overhead, its rays come down to reveal the top half of a steel barrel sunk into the center of the earth floor. In it are ashes from long-ago fires.

In the years before this smokehouse, my father had rigged up a six-foot-high crossbar out in the open from which to hang hams for smoking. But a crosswind might blow the smoke away from under the meat, and the open fire would be more difficult to control.

On one occasion, when everything seemed to be fine, Dad strolled over to the neighbors on the next farm, leaving the hams from two butchered pigs curing in the smoke. Not long after his departure Mother glanced out the kitchen window and saw the eight hams dropping, one by one, into the suddenly flaring-up fire underneath. She called for my father, but when he did not come, she quickly telephoned the neighbors. He came running down the trail as fast as he could and salvaged that summer's meat supply. Only a little charred meat needed to be trimmed away.

Another kind of contrivance and another near disaster occurred just a mile away at my grandparents' home when my mother's folks first settled in Canada from Minnesota. They smoked meat in a large wooden barrel, with both ends removed. Pieces of meat were suspended within the barrel, which was then placed over the short stovepipe-chimney that protruded from their sod-roofed house.

This time, the barrel, with hams inside, caught fire, and Grandmother ran out of the house, waving her apron and hallooing loudly to attract the attention of Grandfather, who was plowing in the field. He came running, too. A neighbor from a short distance away who had noticed the flames also came running, bringing two sloshing buckets of water, and the two men put out the fire without further damage.

These incidents occurred in spring, for that was the season to smoke hams. Pigs of three to four hundred pounds were butchered in late fall, and the hams were cooled and salted down—rubbed generously with salt and then liberally sprinkled with it. By spring the salt had impregnated the meat sufficiently so that the hams were ready for smoking. (Farmers' sausages, however, were smoked following the pig butchering, while gold-eyes from the South Saskatchewan River could be smoked any time during the summer. With red-cored willows as fuel for the fire, these oily fish took on a true "Winnipeg goldeye" flavor when smoked.)

Several days were needed to smoke the big hams properly. Care had to be taken to keep the fire smoking, with greenish wood, but not to let it give off much heat. The hams were to be smoked, not cooked! There was a real art to mastering the whole process. Then came the finished product—hams cured to a smoky-tan outward color—tasty even when raw but delicious when fried and served with hash browns. The smoked hams were hung in a cool outbuilding, such as a granary, for the summer— some neighbors stored them within the grain itself. Thick slices were cut from them almost every day for as long as they lasted.

During the Depression we sometimes were forced to sell hams like these to obtain ready cash. At eight cents a pound, one spring's sale paid the fee my sister was charged to write her grade eleven examinations in town after a winter of home study by correspondence courses. Our log smokehouse certainly paid for itself in more ways than one.

The Hayloft

Robert Louis Stevenson, in *A Child's Garden of Verses*, writes of the "happy hills of hay"—the feed stored in the barn's hayloft—in which he played as a boy. In another poem he apostrophizes the ladder leading up to the hayloft door, that entrance to an enchanted world where cobwebs cling and mysteries abide, secure from the glare of every day.

The cool gloom of an old barn has always made a favorite place to play. John Drinkwater, in his "Wagon in the Barn" (a poem in an old grade-four reader), speaks of the high adventure that he and his playmates had by merely climbing aboard a wagon stored there and riding imaginatively for "miles along the lanes." But to climb up into the hayloft is an even higher adventure, apart from the physical altitude. Raising oneself, step by step, up the rungs of the ladder—feeling their press under the arch of the foot, while clinging to the sides with strained arms to boost one's progress hand over hand—one is like a sailor before the mast in uncharted seas, with strange lands heaving into view.

The loft itself can be a sheltering cave to a shipwrecked sailor, a habitation on a lonely desert island. My boyhood hayloft was truly cave-like, dark with little headroom. The center, under the ridgepole, was six feet high—we could stand upright there— but to go from side to side required stooping. The roof sloped right down to the hayloft floor at the eaves: there were no walls.

Because we had to stoop and look down as we walked along, we watched our step and did not trip over the heap of old harnesses or the dismantled pieces of furniture stored there. One window, with dust-streaked panes, let in light palely at the north end, a diffuse grayness that was in sharp contrast to any streaming ray of sun that found entrance through a chink elsewhere, slanting a golden beam downward with dust motes dancing in it.

The window, opposite the outside-ladder entrance, could be used as a second exit. By standing on a backless chair, we could stick a leg through. Then we had a fair drop to the lean-to roof on that end of the barn. But we had found a second way out of our cave and were in the open again. Or, still using our imaginations, we had come on deck once more, onto the forecastle, and were facing a stiff sea breeze.

Romping about on the lean-to roof had an excitement of its own, and I was familiar with these confines and the extended view. I had crawled up to watch my bachelor uncle paint a picture of our farmyard from this same roof. But now there was no ladder set up against the eaves, and we "sailors" had no obvious way of descending. Shinnying up the end wall to the window was not possible. However, we were not overly concerned: we had not yet finished our round of play on the roof.

When we had, we lined up along the lowest eaves and squatted there, looking at the ground below and wondering whether we had the nerve to jump. Standing on the edge in position to go made the height even greater, and we sat down again. But in time one of us steeled himself for the inevitable leap, bending his knees a few times by way of limbering up, and then jumped down—safely. The rest of us followed, some quickly, others looking hesitantly, waiting for the right psychological moment. Then, as shameful landlubbers, we scurried around to the other end of the barn and scampered up the ladder there—aboard our ship once more, or hidden in our island cave.

Our loft, because of its low roof, seldom contained hay—my father preferred to make neat haystacks in the open barnyard.

But there was often another form of cattle feed in it: oat bundles. Most of them were made into tight stacks, too, but some bundles were always pitched into the loft. Eventually they would provide food for cows and horses, to "cheer the herds with pasture memories" (Charles G. D. Roberts, "The Mowing"), but first they provided sleeping accommodation for the harvest crew at threshing time.

It was during one of these times that I had the idea I would like to sleep in the hayloft, too. I didn't smoke, I told Mother (something Dad constantly warned the crews about), and even Heidi—a girl—had slept in a kind of loft in her grandfather's mountain hut, climbing up each night by ladder. "All right," my mother said, after conferring with my father, "you can try it once and see if you like it." The threshers had left by then, and I would have the loft to myself.

I climbed into it several times that day to look things over. The bundles were still spread about for sleeping, and I tried each hollowed-out bed to see which was most comfortable. That decided, I went down to fetch my own bedding. Mother cautioned that I should wait till it was almost dark—there was no point in letting mice get inside it to start gnawing up her pillows and quilts.

Mice! I hadn't thought of them, but I figured we could live together peaceably enough. At least if there was some rustling noise, I would know who was making it. So that evening Mother and Dad accompanied me to the ladder to be sure I was safely stowed away. Then they left.

I had a flashlight with me, and before lying down I shone it round about my "ship/cave." No bats were fluttering among the rafters; no animal's bright eyes glared back at me. There was nothing to do but crawl under my quilt and go to sleep. A horned owl hooted a few times from across the pasture, was answered by another owl, and that call was re-answered. In between the series of hoots, there was absolute silence. The cool night air streamed in through the window, and I dozed off....

When I awoke, the north window looked gray against the blackness of the loft's interior, and I knew it was early morning. I dressed quickly, hoping to be up before my parents, and stared from my lookout. The landscape was as quiet as an unruffled, pathless sea, but when I walked to the house, I left black footprints in the short frosted grass.

Now I had another notion. Sailors descended from their mast-high lookouts on flexible rigging made of rope. A rope, well fastened to a rafter crosspiece and hanging from the loft entrance, would be just the thing to cling to while coming down backwards, my feet braced against the wall. Securing one from our workshop, I mounted the hayloft ladder again, and once inside the loft, calmly pushed it aside, letting it clatter to the ground below. Then I fastened the rope, flung the end outside, and I was descending, step by backward step, hand over straining hand along the rope.

Was I a jolly tar coming down a mast or Robinson Crusoe stepping down the fortified wall around his cave? It did not really matter. The old hayloft was a place of high adventure, and my going into this enchanted world of half-light and mystery, and coming out from those happy hills of hay and oat bundles, was part of that adventure.

III

WORK ABOUT THE HOME

Pancakes

For a growing boy, what could be more mouth-watering than a plate stacked high with freshly made pancakes? When I was young, it was a regular treat. With all the white lard rendered from two 400-pound pigs each fall, there was always fat to fry pancakes, not only on Shrove Tuesday but on other days, too. And, with us, pancakes never augmented a breakfast. They were, instead, the main (and only) course of dinner or supper.

How well I remember the wonderful sights and sounds and smells of each Pancake Day. First, Mother beat up a creamy batter of flour, milk, and eggs in a large stone bowl. *Clupp, clupp, clupp*—the ladle rhythmically slashed into the batter as a little more of one ingredient, then another, was added to get the right consistency. Mother held the bowl encircled in one arm pressed against her apron.

Meanwhile, some finely split wood was burning down in the firebox of the huge kitchen range, and a small high bowl of melting fat was warming on the back of it. Empty plates were waiting in the warming closet and a couple stood on top. When all was in readiness, the pancake frying began, for there would be no letup once things got underway.

With a big family to feed, Mother had to proceed in grand style. She removed four stove lids and kept four pans in operation the whole time, two directly over the fire and two alongside that still received good cooking heat from the nearby flames. With a sizzle, melted lard from the high bowl was spooned into the pans, each handle turned to ensure that the fat spread all the way across. Then with a further sizzle, and a tilting of the pan, enough batter was ladled out to cover the bottom.

Mother was frying pancakes now with a will. The two pans above the firebox heated up faster, and she lifted the edge of one of the pancakes. Yes, it was done on that side and could be flipped over—so, too, the other pancake. A fresh onset of sizzling filled the kitchen, and a little more fat might be spooned around the edges of the overturned pancakes. The pans had heated up quickly by this time so that the two pancakes were soon done and lifted by spatula onto a plate in the warming closet.

Now the four pans were rotated, the empty ones coming off the direct fire exchanged for the other two. While the third and fourth pancakes fried to a tantalizing piebald appearance of golden-brown patches, Mother re-greased the empty pans and added batter. She alone manned her assembly-line production.

Spoonfuls of hot fat spattering in each pan; viscous batter spreading, like expanding ripples, across it; pancakes bubbling slightly in their cooking, ready to be turned over; steaming hotcakes stacked a dozen high, one plate after another: these were the logistics of her meal preparation. Intermittently she had to re-beat the batter, to prevent the top of it from becoming stiff, and get more wood from the porch to replenish the all-important fire. Delicious smells of cooking pervaded the house, as did the not unpleasant bluish smoke from all the frying.

Mother might well make more than fifty pancakes to feed the six of us. Her pancakes had a unique gummy texture—they were hardly porous, not readily shredding into crumbs when eaten. Made without baking powder or soda, they were somewhat like *crêpes suzette* in thickness but never dry. It did not occur to us to butter them; they were so tender and moist.

Nor did we ever eat them with pancake syrup. Instead, there were fruit preserves such as rhubarb, raspberry, or applesauce. Homemade jams from wild fruit, like highbush cranberries or chokecherries, were particularly tasty. Then there were improvised spreads—dips made from brown sugar and cream, for instance.

The act of eating the pancakes gave rise to a great deal of innovation. Our parents, of course, usually ate them flat from the plate, although sometimes two or three at a time, pinching off bite-size wedges with the side of a fork. To children, however, eating is both an adventure and an entertainment, and we rolled up the pancakes, the better to facilitate dipping an end into some clinging preserve and then biting off coils of zesty cake and filling. Or we spread the whole pancake thickly with saskatoon jam, folded it once across, then the remaining half once more, and ate it in hand, a special, scrumptious four-layer sandwich.

We children were all Little Black Sambos, trying to eat at least "169 pancakes" because, like Sambo, we were "so hungry" once we began eating this wonderful food. And for Mother, who

had stood long at the hot stove, amid smoke and greasy fumes, making the pancakes, it was a pleasure to see us eat them. She was like that other mother in Willa Cather's famous story, "Neighbour Rosicky," whose natural expression of affection was to feed creatures—farm animals, or her hungry boys.

As I grew older I learned more about pancakes in the outdoor books and magazines I enjoyed reading. Hardy outdoorsmen called them flapjacks and ate them in prodigious numbers around their campfire and in lumber camps where the cook prepared even more per individual than my mother had. Why, in Paul Bunyan's camp, flunkies had sides of bacon strapped to their feet and skated about the huge frying pan in order to grease it.

The story I liked best—it was more credible—was of a hunter-fisherman in an old *Rod and Gun* magazine. While making flapjacks at an open fireplace, he flipped them into the air and caught them, other-side-up, in the pan. But he flipped one too high and it sailed up and out the chimney. The accompanying illustration showed him rushing through the doorway, arm extended with outstretched pan to catch the far-sailing, somersaulting pancake.

So, fed by such stories (and my insatiable taste for pancakes), I determined that when my cousin and I were old enough to camp at the nearby South Saskatchewan River, we would make pancakes (that is, flapjacks) in a highly romantic and rustic manner. We beat up the batter in the out-of-doors, using spring water and condensed milk and a sprinkling of wild berries. We fried them in a hand-held pan over an open fire in a ring of stones. And having been outdoors all day, hiking in the woods or fishing along the windswept river, we ate the flapjacks with boyish zest.

But they were not like Mother's pancakes. Ours were thick and pasty and sat heavily on the stomach. We could eat just a few—they were so "substantial." When we returned home, we could appreciate our mothers' pancakes all the better. All the sensory appeals that accompanied the making of them—the *clupp, clupp* of the batter, the sizzling of hot fat in the pan, the wafting tendrils of blue smoke greeting the eye and nose—were heightened.

Pancake Day at home was, as ever, a great day, especially for a growing boy. As a personal favor to the reader, I am appending here my mother's simple recipe for this toothsome meal: three beaten eggs, two and a quarter cups milk, one and a quarter cups flour, and a pinch of salt. M-m-m-m!

Dairy Days

After the cows were milked inside the pasture gate, five full pails of milk, with flecks of foam flying off in the wind, were carried to the summer kitchen. There, on a built-in table, stood the cream separator. Just twenty inches high, it funneled the whole milk through its whirling mechanism to give the desired skim milk and cream, while someone turned its crank.

There was milk for drinking and cooking (and feeding the piglets in the pen) and cream for coffee and puddings (and selling in five-gallon cans in town)—nothing was wasted. Yogurt and cottage cheese could be made from the skim milk, and a good portion of the cream was regularly converted into homemade butter.

I had the job of turning the separator's crank morning and evening for several summers. I would sing to myself at work, and doing so made the time pass enjoyably while reinforcing in my mind the lyrics to dozens of popular songs of the day—"Dream Valley," "Chickery Chick," and "Sioux City Sue." The beauty of it for all concerned was that, with the whirring noise of the separator, nobody could hear me. While singing, I gave heed to the flow of cream and milk from their respective spouts into waiting receptacles—an emptied milk pail for the skim milk and a smaller washed syrup pail for the cream.

I was fascinated with how the cream separator worked. Watching Mother scrub out its spouts, tank, and many-pieced "bowl" after each use, I knew that the bowl, a kind of centrifuge, was the heart of the separator. It also needed to be taken apart completely during the cleaning process. The bowl consisted of a cast-iron base, about four inches in diameter, having a hollow spindle in the center. Over the spindle fitted a grooved cylinder, ten thin cone-shaped disks, a jacket, and finally a heavy cast-iron cover, also cone shaped. A nut screwed atop the spindle with a special wrench held everything in place.

This bowl spun at several thousand revolutions per minute as I turned the crank. Whole milk, poured into the tank at the top, entered the bowl, forced its way between the disks, and by centrifugal force separated into the heavier skim milk (flung out to the edge of the bowl and channeled into the lower spout) and the lighter cream (concentrated in the center and forced up to the higher spout).

It was just a matter of physics, but to Mother—who had to dismantle the bowl twice a day, wash all the parts (in the days before detergents), and reassemble them—it was just more home economics, pure and simple. She used a long flexible wire-handled brush on the spindle and disks (and the spouts) and scalded everything with boiling water before she was through. Sanitation, not abstract theory, was her concern.

As I turned the separator's crank, I made sure I was going at an even speed. Turning too slowly gave more, but thinner, cream. With practice I became attuned to the right note of the machine's hum, which told me the desired cream was being produced. The separator had to be up to proper speed before the initial milk even went through it. A valve on the tank was then opened, and the cream (and milk) soon spouted forth. The arc of the cream's flow was another indicator of correct turning speed.

Once separated, some of the skim milk and cream was poured into pitchers for table use. Milk not required for the next meal or two was carried away and mixed with "chops" (crushed grain) for the pigs. Cream, however, had to be stored for later sale or butter making, and in those pre-electrification days that meant "down the well"—the cold storage facility on any farm.

For some years we had a well and pump near the house, and so the cream, in syrup pails or two-gallon peanut butter pails, hung from slender ropes inside the wooden cribbing's dark coolness. In later years the well went dry and the old cribbing collapsed, so we dug a cooler north of the house. Just eight feet deep, but with snow and water shoveled and poured down in midwinter, it kept an icy bottom for most of the summer.

Then about once a week, depending upon how much milk our cows were giving, Mother hauled up the accumulating pails of cream, tasted each one to make sure they were still sweet, and poured the contents into the sturdy, freshly scalded cream can. Before clanking down the friction lid, she stirred the cream about with a large colander-spoon, and it was ready for "shipping" to the local creamery in town four miles away.

Usually our trips to town coincided with the times of shipping, and the twenty-pound can of cream was hoisted onto the back of our wagon. But sometimes it was just not convenient for any of us to go. What to do, for the cream might sour if shipment were delayed? Mother was never fazed. She would hail a passing buggy—an overland trail to town passed across our farm—and perhaps a Fish Creek farmer, unknown to us, would take the cream to town and bring back the can and check. The checks, from two to five dollars, paid the weekly grocery bill.

Three things our grocery list did not include were butter, yogurt, and cottage cheese. Mother made these herself. The last two seemed to appear almost accidentally. With only raw (unpasteurized) milk at hand, it was natural that some should ferment and thicken. Voilà—yogurt! Mother could help the process along by pouring milk, just beginning to turn, into a shallow bowl and placing it on the back of the kitchen's wood stove (if moderately warm) or on top of the stove's warming closet.

The making of cottage cheese simply carried the process a step further. The sour milk was heated very slowly to about 160 degrees Fahrenheit and kept at that temperature until curds (and whey) began to form. Mother usually sliced through the thickened milk to speed up the process. That completed, she squeezed out the curds and pressed them into a bowl, ready to be served for the next meal.

Making butter was a more involved procedure. Some of the cream in the well was deliberately left to sour. Mother poured pails of it into her three-gallon stone dasher churn, leaving enough room for it to slosh about as she plunged the dasher up and down. With time, she moved the dasher more and more slowly as clots of butter formed in the cream.

I said that making butter was an *involved* procedure, but, I suppose, the main involvement was that of the other family members. As a child, I liked to taste some of the sour cream that scraped off above the lid with each plunge of the dasher. This I took up with a teaspoon, then sucked the spoon like an all-day sucker. When Mother lifted the dripping mass of butter from the churn, others appeared, this time with cups in hand. As she kneaded and shaped the lump of butter in a large bowl, they dipped out cups of buttermilk from the churn and gulped it down.

The butter, now slightly salted, might be pressed into one-pound forms or left in large closed jars and then hung down the well. "It was the *best* butter," as the March Hare said in *Alice in Wonderland*, and also fit for any royal slice of bread, as in A. A. Milne's poem "The King's Breakfast."

Actually, our family always dined royally. What could have been finer than healthy skim milk to drink, or buttermilk for variety, or a generous dollop of sweet cream in coffee? Then there were mounds of cottage cheese setting off crisp garden vegetables in delicious salads; butter spread thickly on heavy, substantial wedges of freshly baked brown bread from home-ground flour; and desserts of gelatinous yogurt spiced with cinnamon, nutmeg, or ginger. It was enough to make us sing for our supper—and bless our dear cows.

Wash Days

They that wash on Monday
Have all the week to dry;
They that wash on Tuesday
Are not so much awry;
They that wash on Wednesday
Are not so much to blame;
They that wash on Thursday
Wash for very shame;
They that wash on Friday
Must only wash in need;
And they that wash on Saturday
Are lazy folk indeed.

My mother liked to recite this rhyme, whatever day she happened to wash clothes. Wash Day for her was usually on Monday, but not particularly early. There were always the regular morning farm chores as well as children to be readied for school.

A few things, however, could be readied beforehand. On a farm without electricity or running water, all preparations were manual. First water was pumped at the well and carried by pails to the summer kitchen a hundred yards away. Eight large buckets were needed, but some of the water might come from the rain barrel under the eaves of the kitchen's shack roof. Any floating insects would be skimmed off and the pails then filled by dipper.

Next a fire was started under the huge closed-in cauldron for heating water. It stood at one end of the summer kitchen along with all the washing facilities. Fine kindling from the woodpile fed the fire.

Two other jobs were sorting the clothes and preparing the soap. Our dirty clothes were stored in a "wash-corner," a closet or bin underneath the chimney. The clothes were sorted into six to eight piles, each a washing machineful, depending on their color and griminess. Some might be soaked first or eventually washed twice.

We usually made a supply of soap in the fall from rendered lard and lye. Now a few of these bars were sliced into long shavings and melted down into a liquid soap in a granite pot on the kitchen range. Liquid soap dissolved more readily in the hot wash water.

By mid-morning the actual washing had not yet started, but there had been a lot of walking between house and summer kitchen, summer kitchen and woodpile, and summer kitchen and well or rain barrel. Finally everything was ready: the standing water, which kept the boards in the washing machine from drying out and springing a leak, drained away; a chair placed behind the machine for the operator to sit on; and a bench placed in front to hold two galvanized tubs, one for rinsing and one for collecting the wrung-out wash.

Our washing machine was made entirely of wood except for the fittings, gears, and flywheel. Even the agitator was wood, and it, fastened to the lid, lifted out each time the machine was opened. In went the hot water dipped from the cauldron, the liquid soap, and one load of wash. Down went the lid—a sliding device connected the agitator to a hand lever—and washing could begin.

Mother, now sitting in the chair, swept the lever back and forth, the agitator within swung correspondingly from side to side, the gears underneath slowly turned, and the flywheel outside spun continuously, giving the whole operation an even momentum. Meanwhile the clothes swished about in the soapy water.

Should the washing ever be done on a Saturday (or during the summer holidays) then I, as a sturdy schoolboy, could help. I could split kindling and carry water and the sorted wash. But my principal job was moving the handle back and forth to operate the machine. If one arm got tired, there was always the other, and by leaning back on the chair, I might even spell each off by using my feet and legs.

The thing was not to let the work get monotonous. The small clock brought from the house to time each wash load seemed to tick ever so slowly while I was operating the machine. *Clacky-clacky* sounded the agitator with each back and forth movement of my arm, but when I had worked for what I thought was a considerable time, the clock showed that only three or four minutes had elapsed. I vowed not to look clockward for the longest interval, only to glance anyway and see that no more time had gone by than before.

Then I started singing—the best way to enjoy the exercise and forget about the clock. I sang the popular songs of the day ("Shabby Old Cabby," "In an Old Dutch Garden," "Carolina Moon," and "Hawaiian Sunset") one after another. The lyrics were memorable, and I think that singing them again and again on Wash Days fixed them forever in my mind. I still know the words to several dozens of songs from the 1930s and 1940s.

The dirtiest laundry was washed for fifteen to twenty minutes, and I had other distractions to make the time pass pleasantly. The summer kitchen's open doorway gave me a lookout onto the bright yard and an expanding view across a field to bushes along the horizon. I might glimpse a flicker or goldfinch darting by at close quarters in its course over the lawn or see at a distance a hawk circling amid the clouds above the trees shimmering in the heat.

Of course, the fact that I was operating the washing machine did not mean that Mother was working elsewhere. It meant that the whole washing procedure could be done more quickly. For me, watching it was diverting, too.

With the dirtiest loads, Mother had me stop the machine halfway through, while she opened the lid (to a cloud of steam) to stir the wash about with a stick set aside especially for that purpose. No bit of wash was to be lodged at a bottom corner and not be properly cleaned. This gave me a minute's respite.

When the load was entirely done, I could sit back and watch Mother send it through the wringer. She used the stick again— the water was so hot—to fish out articles of clothing with one hand and start them into the wringer while she turned the crank with the other. They curled into a tub of clear water on the other side. To me, it was endlessly fascinating to watch the clothing or linen fold and refold itself in passing through the rollers while cascades of water streamed back into the machine—a miniature Niagara Falls.

Emptied of clothes, the machine was ready for another load, a dipper or two of fresh boiling water from the cauldron, and perhaps a bit more liquefied soap. The lid was lowered and secured, and my job began once more. Meanwhile Mother was rinsing the wrung-out wash in the clear water prior to unscrewing the wringer from the machine and fastening it to the tub. I could then watch the same wash, refolding itself and cascading down more water, in its second passage through the wringer.

When the last load was washed, I might do the wringing so that Mother could continue with hanging the fresh-smelling laundry on the wash line behind the house. There it billowed in the wind, flapping like many-colored flags, bowing out the line. A Monday's wash had all week to dry, according to Mother's rhyme, but a few breezy hours in bright sunshine was usually sufficient.

Now it was time for me to drain the dirty water from the machine in bucketfuls and dump it outside. Sometimes I carried it to the adjoining car garage, where our Model A Ford stood, to wet down its earthen floor and prevent dust from rising. Then I poured some clean water into the washing machine, so that things would "not be all awry" with a leaking machine the next time. Any last bit of water in the iron cauldron also needed to be scooped out of its round bottom, then that bottom dried thoroughly with an old towel to prevent it from rusting.

The everyday requirement of clean clothing and linen—no matter which day of the week we washed—had become an achievement of pleasure, of many little pleasures, really. There was the arm-strengthening exercise of running the washing machine—to the machine's own rhythmic accompaniment. There was an opportunity to sing, uninhibited, and to watch, unrestrained. There were the smells of hot water and homemade soap and wet clothes, followed by the fresh air inhaled each time we stepped out of the steamy summer kitchen.

Finally, there was the feel and smell of newly washed clothes brought in from the line. Mother carried them inside in huge armfuls and deposited them on table, chair, and sofa, and the whole house smelled fresh.

Saturday Baths

Happy and not so happy—that could describe my own boyhood memories of a Saturday night in rural Saskatchewan. In summer there was a chance of going into town and enjoying the sights, in winter the thrill of listening to a radio broadcast of a hockey game in faraway Toronto. But another activity—the ritual of the Saturday night bath—had its downside from a boy's perspective. To me, it was just another chore after the other chores were done.

And it was a chore! This was no mere turning on of the tap and luxuriating in a hot tub. On a farm with no running water, the water, ice cold, was carried in buckets from the well. On our farm, even water from a well was hard to come by. The well for our cattle, a quarter-mile away, held a reasonable amount of water, but the hand-dug yard well for household use usually began going dry by late summer.

Bath water was a combination of well water heated to near boiling in the kettle on the kitchen range and cold water dipped from the wooden rain barrel. Rainfall was infrequent in those times; therefore, water from that source was not plentiful either. Sometimes our restrictions seemed similar to those imposed upon the French Foreign Legion on desert patrol.

In winter, rainwater was replaced by melted snow, warming in various receptacles on the kitchen stove. Since our baths took

place before the range—in fact, before the open oven door—
the water supply was near at hand. A hooked rug under the
round galvanized tub absorbed some of the splashing, but still
there was no sense in wasting precious water.

From spring through fall bathing was done in the summer
kitchen, the tub now resting on a binder-twine mat (again
hooked by Mother). Here we could splash to our heart's content. If only we had had more water! Our summer kitchen
housed Dad's workshop along one side so that our castoff clothing might be draped over a vise while our bath towel hung from
a wooden trestle, waiting to be groped for by a wet outstretched
hand at the end of the bath.

As a small youngster, I could sit in the tub, with my knees
touching my chin, while flinging soapy water over my back. A
somewhat older sibling might kneel on the ribbed tub bottom
(not too pleasant a sensation) or resort to standing like a
grownup, for lack of room, and washing off with a cloth.

Whatever the size of the family member, the tub had to be
emptied for the next in line. A grownup could simply grasp the
tub by its two handles, carry it slantwise through the door, and
fling the dirty water into the yard or under a tree. A youngster
needed to empty the tub by dipperful first, until it was light
enough to carry.

All of this was a lot of bother. An uncle who stayed with us
one summer thought it might be easier to take an outdoor
shower bath. To this end, he punctured a series of holes, with
hammer and nail, in the bottom of an old syrup pail. This he suspended on the north side of the house, away from the open
yard. Having told us that this area was now "off limits" to us while
he took his bath, he filled his shower pail with water. From
inside we could hear him splashing and singing, as if advertising
the advantages of his improvised shower—all the time standing
alone "under the flying white clouds, and the broad blue lift of
the sky," as John Masefield says in his poem "Tewkesbury Road."
But his feet must have been treading muddy ground before

long, for the experiment was tried only the one time.

The idea seemed promising, however, and some of us occasionally stripped beside the rain barrel, dipped water from it over us, rubbed ourselves well with soap, and dipped out a final rinse. No tubs to empty that way!

Once, as a young man of twenty-four, unmarried and living at home, my father had taken his Saturday night bath by climbing *into* the rain barrel on his family's farm. The barrel was about half full of water after he was in it, and he had had an uninhibited time splashing about and cascading the water over his back. No tub to empty then either—just the barrel!

But Dad rued taking that particular bath ever after. That Saturday night happened to be one of our province's most memorable evenings—for, on May 15, 1909, Saskatchewan's only noteworthy earthquake occurred. It was an extremely strong shock, felt throughout the province (and even elsewhere), and the Regina newspaper carried the headline: "Prairie Provinces Rocked by Seismic Shock; Buildings Totter and People Rush into Streets." In the town of Rosthern, the brick walls of the community hall and the school were permanently cracked.

The quake of course lasted but a few minutes, the very time Dad had been sloshing about in the rain barrel, unaware of being aided in his ablutions by tectonic forces. It happened that Dad was especially interested in just such things—the first book he bought after teaching himself to read (through keeping up with current events from a daily paper) was a huge geographical/geological text (it served us children well when doing our homework decades later). Yet here he was, a student of geology, missing the opportunity of experiencing a rare prairie earthquake—all because of the Saturday night bath.

His chagrin was accentuated after marrying Mother, for she as a girl of nine had vivid recollections of that memorable evening on another farm only three and a half miles away—of a shaking bed to which she and her sisters had just retired for the night (they already had had their weekly bath) and of running downstairs, where her parents sat awestruck, and there seeing the coal oil moving in the lamp and a towel swinging from its hook.

Later, as a married adult, Mother liked to keep her bath time a quiet affair, getting it done with no fanfare or fuss and bother. All at once she would emerge from the summer kitchen, already in a clean dress, without any of us realizing that someone had been taking a bath. Then she would be back at her work as before.

But for Dad and some of the children, there was a memorable shared bath. On that occasion he decided that our Model A Ford needed a washing before being driven to town. The Saturday night parade to the tub by family members would not leave any extra water for scrubbing down a mere conveyance. Well, he knew of a nearby slough where one stretch of shoreline had a firm bottom.

Hither he drove, with the yet unwashed segment of the family on board. Then with the car come to a stop, up to its hubcaps in water, the passengers gleefully descended, in bathing suits, throwing bucketsful of water over the car and themselves, cavorting about the suddenly shiny car, splashing water recklessly from a seemingly limitless supply in what was a rollicking activity. Now from this boy's viewpoint, that was more like it!

I V

FARMYARD CHORES

Moving Out the Stove

Sometime in late April, but more often early in May, occurred
the annual farm ritual of Moving Out the Stove. Now I am referring to farm homes in the 1940s when the stove that got moved
was the living-room heater. It was the life-preserving center of
the planetary network of rooms, hallways, and connecting
bedrooms it served, and, ornamented with chrome-covered
scrollwork for its high calling, performed well.

Our upright cylindrical stove had the name "Western Oak"
inscribed on its front. Whole blocks of wood, unsplit, might be
shoved through its curved door to feed the raging fire within. At
times portions of the stove glowed red, and such a hot fire was
needed in the drafty, poorly insulated houses of those days during the coldest winter weather.

With the advent of spring, however, the warm sun reasserted
itself, melting the winter drifts and making the crocuses spring
up amid the greening grass. What need then for living-room

heaters, when space indoors was always at a premium and the bulky kitchen range could easily supply whatever heat was needed to take the morning or evening chill out of the house? Summer would be a-coming in, and it was time for moving out the heater. Woodshed philosophers say that if the feat could be done without causing undue aggravation to either man or wife (for it included the taking down and cleaning of the stovepipes as well), their marriage was on a sound foundation.

In our household each partner had a reason for feeling a little perturbed. Some weeks previously Mother would have done her spring housecleaning, scrubbing the walls and ceiling of each room, including the living room where the heater stood. Naturally she did not want any excess soot and tar from dirty stovepipes or stray ashes from the heater scattered about the room. Dad felt he was being taken away from needed outside work, what with spring seeding about to begin. There were all sorts of things to attend to—wheat to run through the fanning mill and fields to assess for moisture—a farmer had a right to be busy with farm work, not some menial indoor task.

"Just watch that the pipes don't come tumbling down again as they did last year," Mother said one time as she laid old newspapers in strategic places along the floor.

Dad, already having tracked in some mud (for why take off overshoes just to put them on again each time to carry out the sections of stovepipe), banged with bare hand against a stubborn elbow joint and kept his own counsel.

This was exactly the stretch of pipe that had given all the trouble the year before. It had come apart where he had not been banging it, and the whole thing had buckled and clattered to the floor. Our poor dog, an innocent and curious bystander, had almost been hit. This year when the operation began, Gyp, with some subdued whining and tail between his legs, immediately headed outdoors to safety.

Somehow this time the stovepipes came apart in foreseen and manageable sections and were carried by us children to the nearest field. There we gently tapped the exteriors with lengths of stove wood to loosen the clinging soot within. An iron scraper was used, too. This was noisy and dirty work and the stovepipe edges were sharp, so the job was hard to complete without sustaining a nasty cut.

Meanwhile, Mother and Dad surveyed the results inside. Yes, some ashes and soot had inevitably spilled directly onto the floor instead of onto the scattered newspapers. Still, these could be cleaned up without too much effort, and tempers had flared only slightly. The two partners looked at each other, reasonably satisfied but without saying anything. It was best not to start a conversation just yet and stretch one's luck.

The newspapers were carefully lifted up and their crumbs of soot just as carefully emptied into the heater's ash pan, which had been taken out of the stove. A honey-pail lid, saved for the purpose, was the precise size to close the hole in the brick chimney

where the stovepipe had been, and this was snapped into place. Now the preliminaries were over, and moving out the stove proper could begin.

This main event was really the simplest job of all. A couple of us husky sons grasped one side while Dad took hold of the other, and together we lifted and slid the heater out through the door, on through the porch, and so by degrees, with a few rest stops, down the walk to the summer kitchen for storage. Or a waiting stoneboat might be used to drag the stove to an unused corner of an empty granary. The newly cleaned stovepipes would be stacked nearby.

Now, with a vacated space in the living room, Mother wanted some furniture rearranged. We children eagerly chipped in with suggestions. Dad looked on with a bemused smile. He had no thoughts on these matters, but it made him feel good to yield to his family's harmless and, to him, inexplicable whims.

"Should we try the davenport here this year, or would that be too far away from the easy chair?" Mother would say.

"What about the sewing machine?" my sister would chime in. "Maybe that could be moved to the other side."

"We've never had the pedal organ over here …": so the comments would go.

By evening, after some experimentation, the living room, with all its old furniture, had a new look in keeping with the burgeoning new season outdoors. For this farm family, the spring-summer season had officially arrived, and it had all begun with the ritual of Moving Out the Stove.

So Fowl and Fair

To a farm boy in the olden days, the question of which came
first, the chicken or the egg, was hardly worth considering.
Chickens were in every farmyard in the neighborhood,
patrolling the short grass and scratching unconcernedly for
food. They seemed to be omnipresent, and it was from them
that we got eggs. Naturally, the chickens came first.

Ours was a motley group, largely Rhode Island Reds, but
with a few black hens and an odd white one mixed with the
flock. While rusty red makes a nice contrast with green grass, our
chickens were not striking. Their feathers were not glossy, like
those of some wild birds—magpies, for instance—but rough and
dull. Daily dust baths did not help.

Each day the chickens went through a similar routine. When
someone opened the door of their little log barn, they looked at
the human askance as at some alien creature, but when he no
longer blocked the lighted doorway, they slowly stepped outside.
Each in turn paused on the doorsill, looking first with one eye at
one side of the world and then, slowly turning her head, at the
other half with the other eye. Then with bills slightly agape as if
in disbelief that another day had come, they fanned out over the
barnyard. Soon they were pecking away and picking up bits of
grain or seeds or insects.

If the rooster, the one bright-feathered bird in the assemblage, had not already heralded the dawn, he now crowed lustily—from the ground or the vantage of a fence post. Yes, all was well with the old world after all.

Henry David Thoreau writes in his classic, *Walden*, that the sound of cock-crowing is more remarkable than any other bird's, even that of wild ones. If roosters were indigenous to our woods as they had been in their native India, he says, their cry would be the most famous sound there, and he gave some thought to keeping a cock at Walden Pond solely for his "singing."

Our rooster, his chanticleer duties over, now began his search for food along with his harem of hens. His deliberate pace was halted on finding some tidbit, over which he made much to-do, attracting the hens' attention; and, curious, they began running up, only to have his highness then eat it himself. So the morning proceeded.

Sometime in the forenoon one of us scattered breakfast leftovers for the chickens. Now when the hens came running, their efforts were rewarded with some choice morsel. Or one of us poured feed into their trough or broadcast it for them, calling "Tuk, tuk" to the clustering fowl.

Afternoons were generally siesta time in the chicken yard. There were still insects to catch: a chicken running full tilt after a grasshopper in zigzag flight—leaning first to one side, then the other, with wings akimbo—is quite a spectacle. But many hens were content to dust-bathe and to sit in their "baths" and doze.

With late afternoon the busy yard patrol began again, and some venturesome hen might even wander out of her territory and approach the house. Our dog knew that chickens were not welcome here and would lie in wait, hoping that some wayward hen would but cross an imaginary line he had noted in his doggy mind. Then he would be off in pursuit, and the surprised chicken, partially taking wing and squawking vociferously, would skedaddle to the safety of her home base.

Calm would return, and the fowl resumed their usual activities till dusk brought them all into the henhouse of their own accord. There they sought their roosts—parallel rails nailed across one end, rising in tiers. With one of us closing the door against nighttime predators, the chickens were secure till the next day's dawning began their daily routine again.

Yet one more activity was engaged in by some of the hens every day: egg laying. That was why a farm boy knew that first you had chickens and then you had the eggs they laid. They might lay them at any time, one hen slipping back into the henhouse unnoticed and depositing her egg in the seclusion of the long, partitioned, open-sided box nailed against a wall. Each partition contained a bit of straw—and some strips of canvas in front for privacy.

There was nothing private about the hen's emergence from the chicken barn, however, once the egg had been laid. She would cackle to herself in busy self-importance, and our mother told us she was saying: "I now my egg have laid, have laid, have laid!"

Eggs could be laid elsewhere, too. Sometimes when the nest boxes in the chicken barn did not seem to be yielding all they should, Mother said the hens could not have stopped laying just like that, and we children would have to scout around the barn-yard to see where the eggs were.

Looking for the eggs was a real treat, a kind of treasure hunt. The horse barn usually held a few, perhaps hidden away in the hay of a manger or else within the chaff and straw underneath. One time I found an egg, unbroken, lying on the bare earthen floor, exposed to open view. Some chickens are more casual about this egg-laying business than others.

Most fun was searching the poplar bluff that abutted the chicken yard. There among the undergrowth of snowberry brush might be a whole nest of eggs awaiting discovery. But were they still good? Who knew? We collected them carefully in an empty syrup pail or grape basket and brought them to the house for testing.

In the spring of the year egg laying took on a new meaning.

This was baby chick time—first came the chicken, then the egg, and finally the little chick, which would grow up into a big chicken.

When Mother noticed a hen beginning to brood on an egg or two she had laid, she gathered up the determined fowl and placed her on a full dozen eggs inside a discarded apple box. There the satisfied hen would begin her three weeks of necessary confinement, while we anticipated the moment when little creamy fluffs of hatching chicks would peep out from under her rusty-red feathers.

What a proud show she made when she once again entered the social world of barnyard society with her covey of chicks in a tight circle about her. What protective care she expended on the little ones, uttering her attentive "cluck-cluck" the whole time, busy with moving them slowly where food might be found. They in turn scrambled around her, trying to keep in close, comforting, physical touch with each other, crying their own timid "teep-teep." Let no cavalier rooster come close now.

Some hens did not always experience motherhood so easily. On one occasion a hen had for a day already brooded her

provided clutch of eggs when unexpected company arrived at our house for dinner. There happened to be nothing in the pantry to serve the guests for a hasty meal, so the eggs were quickly reclaimed and served freshly fried, with homemade bread and butter. The bewildered hen had to wait a few days before more eggs could be found for her.

Other hens did not wait on human aid or whim to further their nesting schemes. To brood their eggs unobserved, they stealthily took to the poplar bluff nearby. They were like Thoreau's wished-for fowl, naturalized without being domesticated, living in the wild as their East Indian ancestors had done. Sometimes we were aware of one disappearing into the underbrush when the chickens left the henhouse in the morning. "Ah-hah," we thought, "she's starting a nest somewhere, and she'll soon give all her time to it."

With others, we never missed their absence among the similarly marked chickens. Then one warm spring day, a new mother hen with her band of "teeping" chicks would emerge from the bluff, surprising us and her fellow chickens in this, her proudest moment, and we gazed in admiration at her splendid family.

We all knew that in time the baby chicks would grow and lose their soft creamy down and then sprout ordinary adult feathers. For a while they would continue to sit around the mother hen each night even though they were too big to crawl under her wings for warmth. Finally they could be independent adult chickens, and the cycle would be complete. The chicken and egg (and baby chick) world had gone full circle in sequence for all to see.

Feeding the Pigs

In my early childhood we had a pigpen about twenty by thirty feet in size. It was made solely of dried logs, stacked half a dozen high and partially notched at the corners in log-cabin style. A space of an inch or two between the logs was sufficient for my cousin and me to squint through to observe the pigs eating. Or, better yet, it enabled us to get a proper toehold—we went barefoot then—and clamber up high enough to look down on them. Then we hooked our elbows over the top rail and watched.

Animals have their own distinct way of eating. A horse will look about to far horizons after a few mouthfuls, and a cow will chew her cud with slow deliberation, entirely at ease. But a pig eats with a kind of helter-skelter abandon, a joy in mere function. This creature gives the food, the business at hand, its undivided attention. To us, thinking about one's food while eating it (instead of chatting sociably with dinner companions) may seem a bit gross, but it is after all the natural, logical thing to do, and I am sure it aids digestion.

A pig's bottom jaw is somewhat pointed, shaped like a trowel, and the animal uses it to scoop up quantities of food from its trough, often several scoops following each other in quick succession. This makes chewing worthwhile. Of course some of it falls away alongside the mouth, but pigs are not particular about such things, and a little spillage can easily be stamped underfoot.

All this we viewed from our vantage at the log pen, enjoying ourselves watching the pigs enjoying themselves. What was most interesting was seeing a dozen half-grown pigs feeding at the trough at one time. It looked like a race to see who could eat the most. Then all of a sudden, without apparent reason, a pig at one end would decide to eat at the other end, so would trot there and squeeze into position.

Doing so necessitated all the pigs moving up one place to accommodate the first pig—much like the participants at the mad tea party in *Alice in Wonderland* moving from one place setting to another when the Hatter wanted a clean cup. Then the next pig would get a similar notion, and all the pigs would move up the line again. This would happen several times. To us, in spite of our (by now) cramped toes and tired elbows, it was great entertainment.

Sometimes special treatment had to be given to the runt of the litter when the pigs were very small and nursing at their mother. She would lie on some straw in one corner of the pen where a few diagonal logs and piled-on straw made a sort of roof for her. There she stretched out on her side, her mouth partly open, blowing up little clouds of chaff as she breathed out. Her piglets lay in a row at right angles to her, like plump sausages, getting their meal.

Then one little pig might be left out, perhaps too weak to fend for itself. It would be wrapped in an old sack, carried into the house, and placed in a cardboard box beside the warm kitchen stove. There we fed it by hand, from a bottle with a rag stopper for a nipple. While it fed, it would look up with its little pig eyes and, as it grew stronger day by day, its straight tail began to curl.

It was a cuddly pig in a blanket, a "queer-shaped little creature" grunting away—like the Duchess's pig carried by Alice. Like it, the runt made a "dreadfully ugly child," but with its pink body and shiny white hair, it was altogether "rather a handsome pig." Soon it was back with its littermates in the pen and eating normal fare.

Our pigs usually ate what we called "chops," which was provided by a small mill set up in the lean-to of the barn. The mill was operated by a belt from the pulley of a stationary engine or tractor positioned outside. On milling days, Dad poured pail after pail of wheat and/or oats into the hopper and the ground-up chops accumulated on the floor. The air was full of flour, and he finally emerged from the choking atmosphere, job done, covered in a sifted whiteness—like "The Miller of the Dee"—"mealy cap" and all. But the pigs had their food. A few pails of it were stirred up with just enough skim milk to make a kind of mush, which the pigs relished and grew fat on.

The pigs liked some variety, too, and we youngsters would carry out vegetable peelings and other house scraps for them. Perhaps what we most enjoyed seeing them eat was lamb's quarters, which we referred to, quite fittingly, as pigweed. It grew as tall as we, or taller, so that it took some effort to pull up a bunch of these (to us) tree-like plants.

Meanwhile the pigs were trying to stick their round noses through the cracks of the log pen, where our toes had once been. They knew what was coming. As we tossed the plants over the rail, the squealing pigs jostled about their homegrown spinach, tearing at it, munching up each morsel. They were truly in their salad days and glorying in them.

And we … we were again hanging with our elbows over the top rail of the pen, our bare toes wedged securely amid the logs below, so that we could watch our favorite barnyard animals eat with their usual helter-skelter abandon, giving the food we had provided them their joyful, undivided attention.

Till the Cows Come Home

What Walt Whitman, in "Song of Myself," says of animals in general applies to most cows in particular: "they are so placid and self-contained; / I stand and look at them long and long." Another poet, Robert Louis Stevenson, in "The Cow," writes of the common cow in "the pleasant open air," walking "among the meadow grass" and eating "meadow flowers." She makes wild landscape, by her mere presence there, domestic. The cow, after all, as Stevenson has averred, is "friendly."

Indeed, our farm cows wandered the pasture in a friendly herd, all facing one way in their grazing, then lying down companionably to chew their cud. Red and white cows clustered in the lee of a bush; a black cow silhouetted on a hilltop; a mix of brindled, gray, and solid-color backs and flanks in a line of cows streamed along a well-worn path: these were our daily domestic scenes.

Our cows had unusually feminine names. Of Mennonite heritage, I was accustomed to solid female names of Biblical origin such as Anna, Mary, and Sarah. So were my mother and aunts named. But our cows were different. They were May and Greta, Josephine, Ruby, Redwing, and Linda.

Each cow had her own personality. May was the matriarch of the herd, by reason of seniority—a large cow, white with gray patches and neat, curving horns. A gentle nudge from one of her horns was enough to keep the herd in line: she would not lead them astray.

Greta, another huge cow, did not grow up with the herd but was purchased as an adult animal. For that reason she may have been the most self-contained, always with the herd but not exactly of it. She was stolid and dependable. Her color was a distinct black-and-white, denoting the closest thing we had to a purebred animal, in this instance a Holstein-Friesian. "Friesian" was allied to our own family name (of Dutch lowland origin), and so she was of special interest to us. She had no horns.

Both May and Greta were hard to milk (yet gave an abundant supply), while the others, of younger generation, were "soft" milkers. Josephine had been May's calf and looked much like her but never achieved her mother's great bulk. Nor did she acquire her mother's even temperament. Josephine had a determined character—determined to find the best grass by stretching her head and neck through the sharp barbed-wire fence till the wire creaked with tautness; determined to drink at the watering trough by literally horning her way among the horses. She used her horns, too, to try to unhook the pasture gate. Yet at milking time, she stood perfectly calmly and let down her milk so easily that she was the best cow for us children to practice the art of milking on. She became the herd leader when May grew old and was sold.

Ruby was all red, of medium size, but yielding the most milk of any of them. When newly freshened, she gave a large milk pail and a half of rich, creamy milk. Her value was in keeping with her name, as her name was in keeping with her color. A virtuous cow, she lacked the bossiness to be a leader and did not mind that Josephine assumed the role.

Redwing was Ruby's calf. A slim, skittish heifer, she would in time mature to be much like her mother—solid, calm, and efficient—an excellent milk-cow. Red like her mother, she received her name because of the white swatch of hairs on her forehead, shaped like a wing. The last cow, Linda, was long-legged, black and white, and so unassuming in nature that one would have scarcely noticed her except for her stark coloring. She gave the least amount of milk.

When we wanted the cows to come in for the evening milking, we did not call them by name. Nor did we call the traditional "cobos." Rather, we had an old cowbell hung by its strap on the pasture gate. A swaying of the bell by one of us, or tapping upon it, sent a mellow "tonking" sound across the pasture—where it gained its special resonance, transcribed through bluffs and bushes in the evening dusk.

Tonk-tonk, tonk-tonk, and the cows in some hidden clearing would lift up their heads from grazing, take a last few desultory sideways tears at the grass, then begin their slow, ambling walk toward home, their rotund bodies now swaying sideways with each step. Josephine led, her hoofs *cra-a-acking* under her ponderous slow gait, with the others strung out behind.

At the barn, but still within the fence, Dad had made a smudge because of the mosquitoes. The cows stood within the blue tendrils of smoke, ready to be milked. Mother and Dad and some of the children set out milk stools beside selected cows— each of us usually milked the same cow(s) day after day—and began rhythmically stripping thin streams of milk into a pail.

The alternating *swish-swish* in the empty pail soon gave way to a steady *purr* as the milk rose and the descending streams cut into a frothy cap. The sound had a mollifying effect—the milker

not thinking at all, hands continuing to move as if of their own volition; the cow immovable altogether except for her jaws working her cud.

After milking, the cows remained about the smudge, content with their day, swishing a tail at reconnoitering flies when the fire burned out. A bittern might call from a distant meadow pool or a ruffed grouse drum from a nearby bluff or ducks whistle by in flight overhead. May and Greta, Josephine, Ruby, Redwing, and Linda stared straight ahead, not looking at anything, just standing there in immemorial pose, part of the pastoral landscape. If they did not see anything, we could look at them "long and long" as the evening drew to its close, these docile animals, these friendly, gentle creatures.

Watering the Cows

It was my task each evening around sunset to water the cows. I had to walk to the western edge of our farm, a quarter-mile away, to the hand-dug well, where we watered our dozen head of livestock.

The cattle, ambling there in single file, had provided me with a narrow path to follow. It was worn several inches deep into the green sod. In fact, they had provided two routes, for their clicking hoofs had worn a path around both sides of a stand of willows beyond our barn. The paths then rejoined to continue on through the checkered shade of some aspens before cutting across the open hills of a hayfield to the well.

At the well were two wooden troughs. Here the cattle and horses would gather, nosing the few inches of day-warmed water, while I climbed over the log rails that shut off the well. As I opened the lid to plunge down the bucket, a moist coolness came up from underground springs.

While the pulley hummed overhead, I let the worn rope slide through my hands, then finally released it altogether so that the bucket fell the last distance to the water with a sharp splash. That way it would tip over and fill. I peered down to watch it submerge far below.

When the bucket was half-filled, I began to pull it up: I was not yet strong enough to pull up a full pail. Now the pulley squeaked in rhythm to my pulling down on the rope, hand over hand, reaching up to the sky to draw the water from the earth. The pail ascended in jerks, with water dripping back down.

Finally the bucket swung over the open well—careful now!—while I held it there with one hand on the rope and reached across to catch its handle. A quick swinging motion and the water was safely arcing out of the pail over the rail enclosure and into one of the troughs.

And my feet were still on solid ground—something I thought of with each bucket that I emptied. For the pulley was a kind of balance, with my weight and my strength pitted against the weight of the bucket of water and the strength of the earth's gravity. Once, I remember, I filled the bucket too full: I could haul it up, but I could not swing it away from above the well to empty it until my fourth attempt.

As I began to fill the troughs with ice-cold water, the farm animal hierarchy showed itself. The two horses—spirited Bruce, a dappled gray gelding, and old Tom, a lumbering bay too tall to be sold when a tractor replaced the other horses—pushed the cattle aside.

The horses must drink first, nuzzling the water as if with affection, raising their heads from time to time, indifferent to the impatient cows. A few cows might try to drink, only to be shunted aside by Bruce and Tom. And Bruce might even shunt aside old Tom.

Eventually, Josephine, the leader of the cattle, refused to be pushed aside. Other cows followed suit, butting away the calves and young steers. When the edge of thirst wore off for the veterans of the herd, everyone could drink side by side.

After all had drunk and the troughs were left full for next day, I closed the cover of the "deep delvèd earth" and strolled toward home. The sunset had changed to a dusky afterglow, nighthawks were darting high overhead, and the cattle were once more grazing under the peaceful sky.

FALL ACTIVITIES

A Field of Stooks

To me, a field of stooks remembered will always be more picturesque than a continuous circling row of swaths. A huge swather, generally self-propelled, moves into a field today, and in a short time the grain is down, lying flat on its own stubble. But with stooks, so much of one's life was involved with the end result that the final scene took on added meaning.

First of all the grain was cut with a horse-drawn binder. The binder stood in a corner of our yard and harbored a family of robins each summer, who customarily built their nest on the bull wheel. If there were no robins, then another species of thrush, the mountain bluebird, would use the twine-holder as a birdhouse. This cylindrical container, which could hold two balls of binder twine, had a round hole near the top, which served admirably for the bluebirds' entry. Only after the birds were done with the binder for another year could it be readied for fall use. (One year my uncle had to delay cutting his crop until the robins in his binder had fledged a late second brood.)

Machinery lasted (or had to last) a long time in those days. Our binder, an eight-foot Deering, was used right till my father died, in 1950. A lot could go wrong with it—and usually did. The binder seemed to operate as a sentient being, a cantankerous one now that it was no longer a bird residence, choosing to break down when a farmer could least afford the time to fix it. Although things were often held together with haywire, the cutting of crops proceeded, usually without additional expense.

One expense that *had* to be met each fall was that of binder twine. It came in a sack of six or eight rolls and cost about ten dollars, money a farmer might not have at the end of a summer's expenses before there was a crop to sell. So he went to the bank to borrow the money, though banks then were intimidating places, with counters in closed-off areas behind polished paneling right to the ceiling and employees visible only through wickets, aloof from their customers.

I remember our neighbor coming back from a dusty buggy ride to town, silent and utterly without hope as his crop was ripening and the bank had refused to loan him ten dollars. But his spunky wife grasped the situation when he drove onto the yard and said: "Don't unhitch the horse—*I'm* going to town." No bank manager would get the better of her, not when her family's livelihood was at stake, and she came back with the bag of twine.

So there was a sense of pride when the binder was finally working and loaded with twine and the farmer sat ready on its spring seat. He seemed cantilevered behind the machine, on his high precarious perch, as though he were not really part of it. But in his hands were the reins to the three or four horses in front, and beneath his foot was the pedal operating the bundle carrier. Beside him, in its cast-iron support, stood a bamboo pole, used as a prod to keep the horses pulling evenly. (In the summer months, the pole doubled as a fishing rod.)

Fastened to the binder was a stone gallon jug, filled with cold water. This was not so much to slake the farmer's thirst during the hot afternoon, as he rode the binder in its anti-clockwise course around the field, as it was to provide the accompanying stookers with needed refreshment. If the jug had been stowed away in the shade of a completed stook, then the laborers could not have drunk from it until they had gone fully around the field. The binder meanwhile could make three rounds, thus giving the stookers, as well as the driver, a more frequent chance at a short break from their routine.

Rest and cold water were often the two main thoughts in a stooker's mind. There was the endless bending down, digging one's fingers into tightly packed bundles, then flinging one under each arm in preparation for standing them upright in an inverted v upon the stubble. This was the start of a round stook. A half dozen more bundles leaning upon the initial two completed it. If the binder had left a sheaf of grain untied, then some lengths of grain were twisted into a rope and gathered about the loose pile to make a snug bundle.

Fingertips became sore, arms felt the prickle of briars bound in with the bundle, muscles ached, and perspiration flowed. At the end of the day, ankles were scratched from stepping among the sharp stubble. What was worse was their itchiness from dust and plant oozings from the severed stalks. Back home my mother once sought relief by rubbing her ankles with the stiff brush of a worn-out broom—until they bled.

If the farm owner wanted long rather than round stooks, the stookers had an even harder time of it. Long stooks were simply a row of six or so inverted vs side by side. When aligned north and south, they received the maximum amount of sun and so dried out better should a rain intervene before threshing time.

Sinclair Ross, in his classic short story "Cornet at Night," describes the valiant but futile effort of a musician, unaccustomed to physical labor, trying to stook a farmer's crop. He lasted but till noon. Had he endured the whole day, he might have come back refreshed the next morning, for muscles do toughen up with each succeeding day. I have known farm girls who stooked all day and still had energy enough to get prettied up in the evening and attend a country dance lasting well into the night.

The most enjoyable time for stooking on a small quarter-section farm like ours came after the evening chores were done. Our whole family, including our dog, Gyp, walked out onto the stubble. The day, no matter how hot before, had taken on a coolness then. A vesper sparrow trilled from the fencerow while a mourning dove cooed from a nearby poplar bluff. Perhaps a harvest moon, mellow-orange and slightly out of shape, rose slowly above the eastern horizon. Ducks whistled by in flight, and the afterglow of departing day lingered on for many hours. It was a time for family togetherness and camaraderie.

As I grew older, our crops became poorer. The four years before my father's death were particularly dry in our area, but there was one compensation. My brother and I began to stook with a fork. It was no trick to insert a three-tined fork into the top of a short bundle and, with a turn of the wrist, set the sheaf down firmly, standing alone, its butt binding with the stubble. Other bundles were forked against it. Although the stooks were solid, my father always grimaced when he saw us at work. That was not how he had been taught to stook, and our using forks only served as an ongoing reminder of what another drought had done.

Yet a sparse field of stooks was picturesque, too, not just a crop to be harvested, not just so much grain in the bin or money in the pocket. As we looked across the field and saw the stooks, backlit by the sun and standing each in its pool of shadow amid the tawny stubble, the scene spoke to us of nesting robins and bluebirds, of temporary victory over an unpredictable machine, of aching muscles and thirst and perseverance, of setting sun and rising moon, of family fellowship and finally a good job done. It was indeed a beautiful sight.

Threshing Time

There was a hum in the air. Walking off to my rural school in the crisp morning, I could hear it. It seemed almost subterranean, an undertone welling up from the earth, a part of the world's slow turning. It was constant, like the basal note of a bagpipe, embedding in itself the other sounds of fall—the soft honking of geese high overhead and the desultory *tsip* of migrating sparrows from fence posts along the roadside.

I was never quite sure where the hum came from. Turning my head in one direction, I thought maybe that way lay its source—until I faced the opposite direction. It was coming from there, too. I was bombarded by a stereophonic hum, the sound of what I knew were freshly chopped-up bits of straw hurtling through the blowers of two or three threshing machines or separators just over the horizon. My young-boy's heart beat excitedly. Threshing time was here; I could hardly wait till the harvest crew came to our farm.

On the morning of the day when the threshers were expected to arrive, I walked on to school with quickening step, as if my hurrying would make the day go faster and I could rush home sooner to share in the adventure of it all. My cousin, who stopped by to walk with me, had to keep pace. The "plumy golden-rod" in the ditches had been blooming yellow for some time, as had adjacent shrubbery been glowing in "rich autumn tints"—this was affirmed in our school readers; but to us, only the advent of threshing marked the real fall season. Our syrup-pail lunch buckets swung vigorously as we hastened on our way.

Just as at Christmastime, when we counted the number of sleeps before the big day, so we now checked off the study periods until three-thirty and dismissal. Then it was out the door and striding as fast as we could. There would be no tarrying beneath some shady halfway poplars to drink cold water, pumped fresh at the school into empty jars from our lunch pails. It was walk, walk, walk, faster and faster. The ubiquitous humming filled our ears, drawing us irresistibly along like a siren call. Soon one strain of it, from *our* farm, would predominate and bring us home at last—my cousin was sure to stay awhile.

Now our eyes verified what our ears had known. A general confusion of dust arose from the pasture (Dad preferred the threshing done there so the cattle could use the straw stack as a winter shelter), and from it a golden arc of chaff and straw bits streamed out above the skyline of intervening bushes. Somewhere beneath all this were men and machines, and horses as well, working in a welter of rhythmic noise.

The serrated knives above the separator's feeder chomped relentlessly into bundle after bundle sliding up into the machine's maw by conveyor belt. Inside, the mangled sheaves were tousled and tumbled through rotating reels and vibrating sieves, separating out the precious grain. The whole machine pulsated to the beat, for the various actions were interrelated, one set of outer double pulleys running one operation and connecting belts running another, which in turn ran yet another.

All had impetus from the main belt, strung out in a gigantic criss-cross to a huge steel-lugged gasoline tractor. As the tractor purred, the belts hissed, the pulleys whirred, the knives chopped, the sieves rattled, the reels sang, and the grain rushed through its metal flue in half-bushel dumps into the waiting wagon. And the hum, always the hum of straw in torrents, forcefully leaving the blower, only to land soundlessly many feet away in an accumulating golden mound!

Oil and sweat—that's what kept the outfit going, that and goodwill and camaraderie. The work was hard—unused muscles grew strong again and calloused hands grew tough as leather—but the bundle pitchers and grain shovelers, all farmers from the neighborhood, were not fazed by manual exertion. It was natural that they should work together at this grand culmination of the summer's labors and do their best—with some high jinks thrown in. On one occasion, a man fell asleep on his waiting rack of bundles at the machine. Rather than disturb him, the succeeding men on their racks worked doubly hard to keep the machine constantly fed with sheaves just to see the sheepish look on his face when he finally opened his eyes.

For two small boys racing into the pasture to the threshing outfit, there was always much to see. One rounded rack of bundles stood alongside the feeder, the team of horses in front standing absolutely still beside the mix of whirring belts. Chaff and dust settled on their backs. Standing tall on the load, the bundle pitcher deftly flung each sheaf, top-end first, onto the conveyor. Now with an audience, he seemed to give the bundle an extra twirl before plopping it down, flashing a big smirking grin at us—white teeth in a dust-blackened face—and we felt accepted as part of the crew.

When the rack was empty, the pitcher swept up any loose straw, threw that into the feeder, too, and unlooped the reins. A *tch-tch* from his tongue and his horses were veering away from the separator and trotting back to the field. A shudder from their backs sent the chaff and dust flying, and the rack rattled and bounced over the humpy earth.

Meanwhile, another rack was maneuvered into position at the threshing machine. Some horses were nervous and had to be led there, the agitated horse pumping its head up and down. If it could not be calmed, the driver would swing around so that the other horse stood nearer the pulsating machine. We watched the goings-on.

Then it was on to the grain wagon for us. Clambering up the spokes of the iron-rimmed wheel—it was higher than we were—we stood tall above things and, with our precarious toehold, looked down at the slowly filling box. From time to time my dad moved some of the grain from its accumulating cone under the spout to the far end of the box. He moved each shovelful with a deliberate slowness, a gentleness betokening his care in bringing in the crop. He then cradled some wheat in his hand and, satisfied, looked up at us. "What do you think, boys?" he said.

We tried to imitate him by cupping some of the grain in our small hands—reddish kernels, cool to the touch. We liked to stick a handful into our mouths, not to check its hardness and grade but to chew. We found if we chewed and chewed and did not swallow that the wheat would turn gummy, yielding a farm-boy's chewing gum that could be augmented anytime with another handful of grain.

When the box was finally full and the grain spout shifted to another wagon, we rode atop the load, sitting on the firm grain, back to the yard. There, my dad, having pulled up alongside the open window of a granary, shoveled off the grain, more robustly this time, while we ran off to the house to catch some of the excitement there. The hum of the threshing machine persisted, and there was no let-up in work anywhere.

One of Mother's sisters usually came over for part of the day to assist in preparing the prodigious amounts of food eaten by the crew. For it was not only oil and sweat that kept the outfit going but lots of food, fast on the table or in the field, eaten five times a day. It was surprising how one or two women could cook enough wholesome food in the allotted time to keep seven or eight hungry men fed. Organization was a key—and busy feet and hands.

Yet I know for Mother and Aunt Mary, as occupied as they were, they could still jabber away, enjoying each other's company, and be caught up in the excitement as well. They were not beyond their own kind of devilment either, although it remained strictly an idea, something they laughed at while rushing about the kitchen.

They knew how ravenously the threshers ate—and had to eat, for time was at a premium. So the two women wondered out loud what they might serve to slow things down a bit—if only they dared—and foil the menfolk's busyness: perhaps fried chub or sucker, bony fish that had to be probed for every tiny bone before each bite; extra-long spaghetti, too long to be twirled into mouth-size forkfuls; chokecherry pie with the stones left in, impossible to be gulped down; and coffee at a rolling boil, absolutely scalding to drink.

All the time they were busy serving the foods of the real menu—porridge, fried ham and potatoes, and thick slices of homemade bread for breakfast; for dinner and supper mashed potatoes prepared in huge canning pots, sides of roast beef or pork, myriad boiled garden vegetables, hefty wedges of apple, rhubarb, or saskatoon pie, with drinkable coffee and rich cream, served on an extended table in the dining room.

Mid-morning and mid-afternoon lunches were brought to the separator, to be eaten on the fly by bundle-team men just before or after pitching off their load. Sometimes the threshing-machine operator or foreman would spell them off by taking a turn at "spike-pitching" so that the machine could keep running during lunches (the baseball term "relief pitcher" did not occur to us then). Here, fresh buns with slabs of meat, giant cookies, and fresh ripe fruit, such as peaches and pears, made the fare. A couple of kettles of coffee were needed to fill the cups several times.

So there was always lots of food ready for one meal or another, from which two hungry schoolboys could do some in-between-meal snacking. Often Mother would buy some ring bologna and ketchup to go with her oven-fresh buns for field meals, and for us to eat this "bought" food out at the separator with our heroes from the threshing crew was special indeed. Sure, we had roast chicken and beefsteak and pork chops, regular farm fare in spite of our relative poverty, but to have bologna and ketchup—what a treat! It is still one of my favorite meals.

There would be no threshing after supper, so work continued as long as possible, through twilight and into gathering dusk. It was a scene of luminescent skies and silhouettes. The separator seemed to bulk even larger as a solid black object against the orange glow when one could no longer notice all its mechanical intricacies. But the belts were still whirring, the machine still digesting its diet of bundles. All sounds of the process gained resonance in the cool of evening, no longer the clattering of individual parts but rather a blended sonorousness, somewhat muffled in the night air, with the blower's hum still distinguishable.

Then the last rack was unloaded, the last bundles pitched into the machine. A few last straws hurtled from the blower, a last dump of grain landed in the box, and the foreman at long last turned off the tractor engine to end the day's labors for man and machine, and horses, too. The main belt slowed markedly, the many separator pulleys it drove lost momentum, and just like that the whole operation came to a wheezing stop.

Silence. Nothing to hear—although for a brief time it seemed as if the humming still persisted—as if the machine had been turned off but our ears had not. And then the lesser sounds of night, present all along, came flooding back, registered on our hearing—the wind in the dry trees, the crickets' chirring, and the far-off hooting of an owl—and we became attuned to a quieter world.

"I guess we've got her done for another day," the bundle pitcher announced from his rack as he drove to the barn to unhitch his team and feed and water the two horses. The other men had already completed these chores and were trooping to the lamplit house for their supper. But first it was time for a general wash-up, something they did not bother with at noon.

An upended apple box stood outside the front door with a

granite basin, some castile soap, and an old towel. A bucket of warm water was nearby. Each man in turn slathered his face and hands with soap, sloshed himself with water, and then flung the basin of water across the grass so that the next person in line could begin. To complete his grooming, he ran his wet fingers backward through his hair several times.

With the men seated at the table, Mother again served up mounds of food, the men falling to with the usual relish. But they ate more leisurely now, occasionally contributing a remark if Dad or the foreman started some conversation. I was all ears, of course, cherishing every syllable spoken by these stalwart sons of the soil. Mother asked particularly about their wives or children—and was responded to, however briefly, with a kind of rural gallantry.

The meal over, the men filed out quietly to take a last look at the clouds or stars (and so gauge next day's weather), perhaps to have a last smoke, before crawling up into the barn's hayloft for their night's rest. Oat bundles spread out on the loft floor were the mattresses on which they heaved their bedrolls of coarse blankets—sleeping bags were not in common use. Below them they could hear their own horses, stamping on the earthen floor, nosing about the mangers for another mouthful of oats.

It was my bedtime, too. Pictures and sounds of the day lingered in my brain as I dozed off beneath snug sheets and covers—the high tottering racks of bundles pulled by what looked like diminutive horses in front; the synchronized mechanics of a running separator; the banter of men in the field and of women in the kitchen; the abundance of food; the golden-red grain, focus of all activity, heaped high in the bin; and everywhere, always, the humming, the pervasive hum of the separator, the far-carrying note giving voice to autumn and heralding its grandest adventure. Next morning I would hear it again as I walked off to school and would follow its siren call home once more.

POSTSCRIPT: Before I reached my teen years, I stayed home from school at threshing time to be part of the "crew"—to shovel grain into the open window of the granary with Dad, matching his every shovelful, scoop for scoop, as we emptied the wagon box, although my scoops were far smaller than his. Then, at age sixteen, I worked with my brother as a joint pitcher on a bundle team, loading up in the field, then feeding the insatiable separator. The hard work, exhausting to be sure, did not diminish my earlier boyhood sense of adventure that marked "Threshing Time."

Bundle, Rack, and Stack

Many signs of fall were coming to the farm. Already in August sandhill cranes from distant tundra marshes passed high overhead on their migration southward, gliding in swift black Vs; their *k-r-r-oo-oo*'s a far-carrying lonely call borne through the crisp air to us earthlings below. Local crows, from their treetop roosts, streamed out across the sky each morning toward daytime feeding grounds and flapped back in a seemingly unending wavering line at dusk. The trees that harbored them, aspen and balsam poplar, were fast becoming yellow and tan—or leathery brown from early frosts.

All around us, Keats's "season of mists and mellow fruitfulness" ("To Autumn") held sway—from small insects rising up cloudlike in the warming sun to crickets singing in the grass to darting swallows twittering about the barnyard. By month's end the ripening grain, tawny-gold, was harvested, the quintessential sign of fall.

One crop, however, escaped the "winnowing wind" of threshing machine and storage on "granary floor." Oats, cut and bound green, then stooked, were reserved for cattle feed, head and stalk. Cured in the field, they were hauled home to be stacked in the barnyard. At our farm the activity was enjoyed by man and beast, to the accompaniment of cricket and crane, crow and swallow, in an autumn-colored world.

Early one morning Dad stuck a three tined fork upright in the hayrack to announce the event, the curved tines wedged into a crack between the floorboards, the handle ready to be grasped in loading bundles afield. The first to notice it was our dog, Gyp. Going for oat bundles marked his favorite day, and he immediately lay down under the rack so as not to miss any of the proceedings.

While Dad finished his barnyard chores and continued on to the house for breakfast with the rest of us, Gyp never moved. He would miss his own breakfast that day in his keen anticipation of sniffing under each upturned stook as the bundles were pitched aboard the rack, perhaps catching a vole or two, and generally exulting in the family outing.

It was indeed a family event. As a small youngster, I could ride in a feed box fastened to the back of the rack, lying backward, with my arms and knees hooked over the sides. My job in the field was "not to get in the way," but to step aside in the sharp stubble. No one said I could not watch and learn in all the excitement, running along with Gyp. He wagged his tail continuously, always eager to be off to the next stook.

Bruce and old Tom, the horses pulling the rack, seemed to enjoy their day, too, and on these occasions worked well together. After ambling out to the field with the rattling hayrack in tow, they paused at the first row of stooks to be loaded. Now there was no hurry. Tails swished at reconnoitering flies; muzzles snitched at some late green growth among the stubble. Then after the first few stooks were pitched aboard, a *tch-tch* from Dad sent the team walking slowly to the next stooks in line, there to have another short rest.

The procedure was different from that of the frenzy of threshing time. In hauling oat bundles for feed, each family worked at its own pace, taking time to look up into the sky for birds or to scan far horizons for their wealth of colors. The air had a scent of fall in it, and one breathed deeply.

I think of the ease depicted in John Constable's painting "The Hay Wain." The farmer has paused with his empty rack amid a stream where the horses can have a refreshing drink before continuing into the distance for another load. A black and white dog, like Gyp, watches from the water's edge, and peaceful clouds fill the sky. Despite the hard toil, rural life held its golden moments in faraway England in 1821, the time of the painting, as much as it did in my boyhood.

When I got older, Dad presented me with my own pitchfork (it is still a proud possession, my initials carved in it from long ago). Now I could load bundles along with the rest of my family—of course, according to my growing strength and ability. Dad usually remained on the rack to build the load, particularly after the rack was half full.

All bundles along the two sides had to lie with their butts outward, the sheaves in between stacked in tightly. As the load grew higher and higher, Dad, on top, shifted each thrown-up bundle, making sure the miniature mountain was balanced. Sometimes the last bundles of the rounded load were a few feet above the top of the hayrack.

Then began the slow journey to the barnyard, Bruce and

Tom pulling steadily, the load tottering slightly as it proceeded over the uneven field. Riding high on top gave me the feeling of being aboard a sailing ship on a slightly heaving ocean, at one with "the lonely sea and the sky," as in John Masefield's "Sea Fever." The creaking of boards in the hayrack and of the horses' harness could well have been that of a ship's timbers and rigging.

At the barnyard, where the stacks were to be made, Dad was the first to climb down. Two of us remained on the rack to throw down the sheaves. Dad was very particular about each stack's construction. It not only had to be tight and capable of shedding rain but also had to give the appearance of being able to do so. Furthermore, it had to be symmetrical: he did not want to look out of the window each morning and see a stack he had made askew against the skyline. That would have spoiled his whole winter.

So the sheaves were carefully laid in a perfect circle for a foundation, butts extending outward again, while he, like a master stonemason, proceeded to build an upright circular wall, interlaying a maximum number of bundles inside. As his stack grew higher, our rack of sheaves grew lower, then empty, sending us all back into the field once more, with Gyp loping happily along within the hayrack's shade just behind the rear axle.

Again the horses stopped at a row of stooks while we pitched on fresh bundles, then moved on at the sound of Dad's *tch-tch*. If Dad was pitching bundles onto the near-empty rack and the horses needed turning to the next row of stooks, he simply used his fork to depress one rein behind the horses' rumps (the free ends were tied to the rack), and the team headed in the desired direction. We continued filling the rack.

The bundles were not tossed on haphazardly even though Dad had climbed back on top to arrange things. Field pitchers were skilled in forking up a bundle, tines near the butt end, then arcing the fork, tines downward, so that the bundle was released in exactly the required position. At threshing time experienced field pitchers singly built up such flawless loads.

Once more we were back in the barnyard, pitching bundles to Dad on the stack. Only now, we would eventually be throwing bundles *up* to him as the rack emptied and his elevation increased. To finish a stack, he decreased its circumference, building the top into a roof-like cone. Then one of us set up a ladder so that he could crawl down.

Our journeys to and from the field continued through the day. Mother left us sometime in mid-morning to prepare dinner, which we ate heartily when noon came, as did Gyp, who fell to vigorously at his own plate on the floor. The contented horses, unhitched, had a good feed of oats at the barn. The best meal was the mid-afternoon snack, eaten at the stack or out in the field, sitting against a stook. We all loved picnics, Mother especially, and food eaten outdoors always had a real zest.

We relaxed completely, our legs stretched out in the stubble, attending only to what we ate and other sensations of the autumn world about us. Cranes were still calling their soft rolling *k-r-r-oo-oo*'s, although sometimes we searched vainly for their outlines against the sky. They were simply too high to see in all that blue. The world seemed infinitely large, and our souls expanded in that immensity. The sun was warm upon us, and we felt at peace with things.

Then it was back to our pleasant work, with the sun's light mellowing in those shortening days of fall. The horses continued with their brief intervals of rest between pulls and Gyp with his nosing of laid-open stooks as if each one were the very first investigated that day. For us, it was a load of pitched-on bundles hauled home, and another and another, and finally the last load of the day—a bringing in of sheaves for yet another year. The sun was setting, but the day was warm enough for the crickets to persist with a faint chirring along the field's edge. Tiny insects danced crazily in golden-flecked swarms in the late light, and swallows skimmed effortlessly through the sky. Crows winnowed homeward to their nighttime roosts.

Yes, we were bringing in the sheaves, as the old hymn says,

but that hymn has a triumphant marching air, totally inappropriate to the mood of our easeful, slow-moving hay wain in the quiet prairie evening. More fitting are the music and words of another hymn (by Joseph Barnby and Sabine Baring-Gould):

Now the day is over;
Night is drawing nigh;
Shadows of the evening
Steal across the sky.

Keats's ode to the season affirms this kind of music—"While barred clouds bloom the soft-dying day"—and it is echoed by our own Canadian poet Charles G. D. Roberts in his depiction of another rural scene in "The Potato Harvest": "Down the hillside / Lumbers the wain; and day fades out like smoke."

Sawing the Winter's Fuel

A large pile of wood, sawed into stove-length pieces during the late fall, gave a warm feeling of security for the coming winter. Our woodpile stood in the center of our farmyard, dominating the scene, as though it were the most important feature contributing to the life there.

In Indian summer we hitched a team of horses to haul the logs from dried trees in our pasture to this spot. Our ten acres of poplar bluffs did not always yield enough wood each year, so my father and older brother, Ernie, sometimes hauled logs from farms east of us along the South Saskatchewan River near Batoche. They might pay a few dollars for each load, which they had to chop first, or they might haul one load of logs into the owner's yard for every load they hauled into ours.

Then, perhaps in November and sometimes after the first snowfall, the logs were sawed into one-foot lengths that would fit into our kitchen range and living-room heater. As a boy, my job was to throw the short lengths away from the saw as they were being cut. My brother, or sometimes my mother, dragged the logs to the saw, which we had borrowed for the occasion. It had a circular blade more than two feet in diameter, mounted on a frame. A belt from a pulley on our Fordson tractor supplied the power.

Dad stood at the saw and repeatedly pushed each log into the open whining blade. I stood right next to it and grasped the end of the log being sawn off, carefully watching its journey into the biting blade until it was severed. Then I threw the piece of wood over my shoulder to form that year's woodpile behind me.

All day the blade sang its high-pitched whine. The sound rose in pitch as it cut relentlessly through the log, and ended with a twang, as from a giant tuning fork, when the log came free. "Whir-r-r—whine—twang! Whir-r-r—whine—twang!" The noise tore at my brain, even as the blade sliced into the log. Always my gloved hands were no more than a few inches from the whirling saw.

I could never cease my concentration—watching my hands; watching the blade; throwing the wood away; grasping the log again; always reaching to the blade, but never too close: watching, throwing, grasping, as the pile of logs diminished and the pile of wood grew higher behind me.

Sometimes the blade might strike a knot, and the log would have to be jerked back so that the saw would not get stuck and stop. Here was a break in the monotony—the saw would sing at a different pitch for an instant. But the log end might twist and one's hands might come even closer to the fatal blade. Or the belt might come off the saw's pulley. Then one could step back and relax for a minute.

When the logs were so big that I could not throw the sawed lengths away, I merely thrust them aside, making sure that they rolled far enough away not to trip me. And as the pile grew behind me, I had to be on guard for pieces rolling down the pile toward my feet.

Any farm community can tell of accidents that occurred when sawing wood. I can recollect two men who were killed by falling into the saw. And I remember my father once falling down at the saw while I was throwing the wood away. He had had a dizzy spell, but as it came upon him, he realized that he must fall backward to save himself. Dumbfounded, I saw him waver, then fall harmlessly into the snow.

In a more striking incident, one that has parallels to what Robert Frost records in his poem "'Out, Out'—," I was witness to a father and son driving hurriedly to the doctor in town with a horse and stoneboat. The youth was dancing up and down in pain, one hand bandaged in cloths spotted with blood.

One can imagine, then, my relieved feeling at the end of another year's sawing. The air was suddenly so still—no more ringing in my ears from the saw's persistent whine, no more sawdust flying up into my eyes, no more steeling myself to be alert. Then there came a rush of little sounds that had been drowned out before but now were magnified: the wind in leafless pasture trees or the twitter of a small bird's wings in flight.

Before me was a winter's supply of wood. It was a pleasure to engage in the safe work of throwing some of the wood lying around the edge higher up onto the pile so that it would better shed the rain and snow. The day's tense occupation could be more or less forgotten for another year.

Snowy Woods and Bitter Cold

A jigsaw puzzle my cousin and I liked to pore over on a winter's evening showed a sturdy woodsman walking through blue snows at dusk. He was dressed warmly in felt cap, snug scarf, heavy capote, thick trousers with stockings pulled over them to the knees, and stout leather moccasins. Gauntleted mitts covered his hands, one of which carried a small camper's axe, and bearpaw snowshoes were on his feet. And it was cold, for the man's breath hung in the air; it seemed we could hear the crunch of each step he was taking.

As the picture took shape before us, another grim circumstance, besides the deep snow and bitter cold, confronted our woodsman. The grayish outline of a great-pawed lynx began to appear, piece by piece, upon an evergreen limb above the unsuspecting walker of the snows. It was crouched to spring, the muscles already flexed in its legs, and as further inserted pieces revealed, its yellow eyes glowed menacingly in an inscrutable face while its short tail tipped upward in anticipation of a surprise assault.

Each time my cousin and I assembled the puzzle we wondered afresh about the man's fate. Would the lynx really jump? Would the man leap aside at the last instant? Would the little camper's axe be sufficient weapon to ward off the attack? Would the man get back to the safety of his cabin that night—injured or otherwise? There was no end to our questions.

Our romantic dream of life in the wintry wilds was nurtured by the puzzle, and that was the reason for putting it together again and again. My older brother joined our boyish speculations by saying that he thought the lynx, like most animals, would instinctively fear man and therefore remain hidden in the tree. His opinion carried some weight, for after all, it was *his* puzzle, but still we were not entirely convinced. Our dream of northern woods with snow-laden trees demanded at least the possibility of a lynx attack, of wild nature asserting its true dominion there.

To me, our farm world in the Saskatchewan parklands was, just then, sadly deficient in wild animals—there were no lynx stalking woods with snowshoe paws, bears hibernating under snow-concealed brushwood dens, and moose yarded up in icy drifts amid the trees they browsed. When, later, I did see a lynx on our farm—it had come down from the north as these animals do during the cyclic decline of rabbits—it skirted the corner of a bush so deliberately and unconcernedly, giving no heed to us, that it suggested no wild creatures had lost their native rights even here. My cousin and I reassembled our old jigsaw with renewed interest.

Any picture of the north woods fascinated me as a boy, whether it was the painting on a Hudson's Bay Company calendar sent to our rural school each year or the F. V. Williams pen-and-ink drawings illustrating stories in old *Rod and Gun* magazines my uncle left at our house. They spelled romance, and I studied them long, trying to resolve myself into them. The artist, with a few strokes of his pen, could indicate the great depths of snow in his winter scenes and, with a few more dabs here and there, show some furtive animal tracks across the white wastes outside a forest's shelter. Maps of the north, with place names like Snowdrift and Trapper's Inlet, engaged us in what one writer happily called "map-dreaming"—this while I sprawled on the floor beside the glowing hot living-room heater.

When I was outdoors, away from the farmyard, I imagined myself in some northerly locale, braving the elements. A snowstorm was energizing, and I longed to be enveloped in its gray world, floundering through the drifts, trailing homeward to some cabin in the woods. Once I built a lean-to of branches in the middle of a poplar bluff and envisioned myself huddled in it overnight, keeping a fire blazing in front while unseen woodland animals eyed me with curiosity. That would be as cozy as lying before the heater.

My uncle Hank, no doubt, was largely responsible for promoting some of my boyhood winter dreams. He had gone up north to homestead in the Meadow Lake country before the Depression years; then, to earn extra cash, he had ventured farther north, into the deep woods, running a trapline for several winters. It was an exploit of the greatest daring to my mind, his packing in supplies for a whole season's trapping, going whither no man knew. At his "destination" he built a log shelter, complete with parchment window, his own snug harbor in the woods. Horned owls hooted from the overhanging trees, and tracks of mink and otter and fisher encircled his hut and led to a nearby lake.

What stories Uncle Hank had to tell us when he got back, perhaps with a load of frozen fish to sell, to stay a few nights at our home. Now he had someone to talk to again, away from the silence of the north, and he knew he had an eager audience in us children. Yet he seemed to narrate his adventures almost incidentally, as afterthoughts to some conversation with Mother and Dad. How could he be so casual about these breathtaking experiences?

One incident that he eventually related occurred while he was on the trail for an extended time. He had had to improvise a shelter or windbreak and build a fire. Carefully he nursed along the sputtering flames as with numbed fingers he fed the blaze with broken twigs, then larger branches. Ah, the welcome heat soon flared out in all directions, the flames dancing higher than his head. But most of the heat escaped upward, for a few feet sideways the bitter cold formed an encircling wall. He had to slip through this icy barrier many times to secure bigger and bigger logs to keep the fire going.

Then he luxuriated in its warmth, resting from his arduous walk earlier in the day and his immediate scrounging for fuel. The flames were so pleasantly warm, the sounds of their flickering so reassuring, their dancing and sputtering so hypnotic to watch, he could hardly keep his eyes open. So tired ... His head dropped lower, swayed slightly to one side as he fought to keep awake—mustn't fall asleep ... keep the fire going. His head dropped lower still, and, the warning signals deep within quieted at last, he slept soundly while the fire burned slowly down, slowly crumbling to mere embers, and went out. The circling wall of winter's cold swept over him.

A squirrel's excited alarm broke his sleep. That chir-r-ring/chattering in his brain—what was wrong? He shook himself and then was fully awake to the scolding from the little red rascal on the tree overhead—and to the penetrating cold. He could hardly stir. But his mind was fully alert to the situation, and he struggled to renew his fire. Numb fingers refused to obey his will, but he had to have warmth.

His actions were deliberate now, his self-directed commands loud in his brain—mustn't hurry, mustn't panic, get a match lit, shield it within the other hand (then, the match slipping away, hissing out in the snow); once more, concentrate, concentrate for very life, fingers—don't let go, just don't, now some curled birch bark (there, a little fire); add some little twigs, more twigs, don't hurry, don't panic, keep the flame alive, shield it, more twigs: the soundtrack in his mind was on rerun, and the sputtering flames, nursed along, soared upward, and at last became a full-fledged fire. Uncle Hank always maintained that the squirrel with its propitious chatter had saved his life.

My uncle's stories, plainly, were as good as any I read those days about the romance of snowy woods and bitter cold. And I read many. Our school readers had stories by Charles G. D. Roberts of adventures in backwoods lumber camps, where bears awakening from hibernation prowled the deep snows. The farm weekly we subscribed to carried a serial—Philip H. Godsell's *Arctic Trader* (1934), an account of twenty years with the Hudson's Bay Company at isolated posts on Canada's frozen frontier.

My favorite, perhaps because it somewhat paralleled my uncle's career, was Tony Onraet's *Sixty Below* (1944). Onraet had set out to the north at roughly the same time as Uncle Hank had left for northern Saskatchewan. Only Onraet had gone much farther, into the Northwest Territories to Great Bear Lake. The romantic-sounding chapter titles in his book, such as "Husky-Dogs," "The Northern Lights Dance," and "The Empty Lake," further enhanced my view of wintry wilds. His vivid writing gave not a rosy hue to things but a bluish cast—the cold blue of tree-shadowed snow. This was the true romance of the season—its great cold and enveloping snow. And the title, *Sixty Below*, is a wonderful phrase to encapsulate all that winter is about. One frosty morning at our farm home, Dad awoke early to check the thermometer and reported back to the rest of us still in our warm beds: "Sixty below!" There was pride in his voice as he gave out the news, and we all savored our situation.

So let the snow fall; let the cold crunch down. The romance of winter was ever alive in all of us—not in just one adventurous boy doing jigsaw puzzles or poring over northern maps and pictures or imagining himself trekking through snowy woods—so long as the pressing cold and snow really asserted themselves, showing that nature had lost none of its primal vigor yet.

Winter Evenings

Evenings on the farm were always a special time, particularly in winter. Coming in from the last of the outside chores was a retreat from the ever-present cold, and our family finally gathered in the warmest room of the house—the living room—for the long hours before bedtime.

Winter evenings, of course, were long. At that time Saskatchewan was on Mountain Standard Time, and the sun had already set before four o'clock during the shortest days. The coal-oil lamp on the table might be lit before we came home from school.

The evening proper began after supper and after the cows had been milked, the dishes washed, and the cream separator, just used, scoured out. Dad stoked up our "Western Oak" heater with blocks of wood—sometimes its undersides glowed red with the burning of a knotty, sap-filled piece of fuel—and most of us had to keep our distance to be comfortable.

My favorite spot was on the floor in front of the heater, watching the darting flames through the mica-plated stove door. A hooked rug underneath kept me from the cold of the linoleum, and an old coat pushed against the bottom of the door leading into the porch kept drafts away. My parents and older sister and brothers sat about the table with a newspaper or else lounged on the davenport.

Evening activities were varied. Dad sometimes read Mother a continued story from a farm weekly while she darned a sock or two. "A man's work went from sun to sun, but woman's work was never done" was ever the maxim. Mother's evening activity, for at least part of the evening, was simply another form of work. But, no doubt, she was glad to be sitting down and having all her family about her.

On other occasions Dad might start a game of solitaire—his thumb going to his moistened lip each time before he deliberately laid down the next card. But he liked an audience, and Mother enjoyed pointing out moves he had overlooked. If the game seemed to be coming to a successful conclusion, we children would gather round as the final plays evolved.

Usually, listening to the radio was the main focus of a winter evening's entertainment. After all, this was still the golden age of radio. What exciting fare there was, and what stimulus to our imaginations only to hear the programs and form the pictures in our minds!

Our radio was powered by a "battery-pack," and we never listened for more than an hour and a half at any one time for fear of running it down. This made listening to the radio a privilege, and we sat around the set and shared the excitement.

Sunday night brought us "Jack Benny," "Edgar Bergen and Charlie McCarthy," and "Fred Allen." Some adventure was

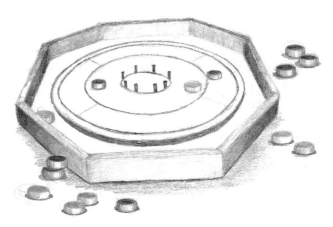

always enacted with gags carried over from previous weeks. We anticipated this running humor, looked forward to it each time, and laughed anew whenever we heard it. Guest stars added variety.

On Monday was "Lux Radio Theatre," a dramatization of current Hollywood movies, under the direction of Cecil B. DeMille. Although we only went to movies on an odd Saturday night in summers in town—where the runs were mostly B Westerns—we were well acquainted with the best that the film capital had to offer: "Casablanca," "The Petrified Forest," and "Maytime." Also we got to know the various actors and actresses almost as personal acquaintances, for they spoke a few words directly to the radio audience when being interviewed by DeMille for some minutes after the performance.

Tuesday was a particularly good night, with "Amos 'n' Andy," "Fibber McGee and Molly" (remember his hall closet?), and "The Bob Hope Show." We laughed at the antics of these comedians then discussed and chuckled over them during the rest of the week with neighbors at work and fellow students at school.

So through the other weekdays (Thursday providing musical comedy entertainment with Bing Crosby), until Saturday brought Foster Hewitt's "Hockey Night in Canada." His "Hello, Canada and hockey fans in the United States and Newfoundland" was heard in thousands of farm homes across the country. Since the hockey broadcasts followed only the Toronto Maple Leafs, we came to know the players, again almost as personal acquaintances, as we listened to their on-ice exploits. Perhaps because the radio broadcast gave free rein to our imaginations, hearing the names of present-day hockey heroes never creates quite the same rush of excitement as hearing "Syl Apps," "Gordie Drillon," or "Turk Broda." (Apps, the Leafs' captain, was one of my boyhood heroes.)

Meanwhile, we had our own games to keep us entertained, some chiefly reserved for occasions when guests called. "Bingo" was new in our district then and was a favorite standby for a time.

Who could have thought that half a century later our cities would have huge bingo halls needing government regulation, with advertisements in daily newspapers?

Table tennis was a more active amusement. Many a dining-room table had extra boards inserted into it to facilitate play. At our home, once the table had been extended, someone got the notion to use the surface also as a kind of improvised "pool table." Books or old catalogs lined the edges in place of side cushions, with openings where the pockets would ordinarily be. Spare table-tennis balls, appropriately marked, served as pool balls, while a couple of yardsticks were the cues. Farm children were adept at "making do" when it came to amusing themselves.

Perhaps the favorite game was crokinole. Our parents had played it as children, and probably their parents before them. Four could play at once, and their play was a good spectator sport for the others as each side shot its checker-like disks at the opponents' blocks through a ring of pegs. The winners could be challenged by two of the spectators, and this procedure was repeated many times through a whole evening.

A final activity was singing old favorites around the pedal organ. Mother was the organist in our family, although some of the children later manifested her talent. No matter who played, it was easy to sing harmony to such songs as "Love's Old Sweet Song," and "Memories." As our singing filled the room, there was a feeling of family togetherness and good fellowship. Later there would be cocoa and cookies.

In the course of the night's entertainment, we had been in touch with the exotic outside world through wonderful radio, had actively participated in our own entertainment, and now sensed an inner well-being as we came to the end of another winter evening on the farm.

Rural Skating Rinks

Not only during the Great Depression but also in the decade following, water was hard to come by. Wells went dry, alkaline sloughs became dusty flats, and any spring runoff was immediately soaked up by the parched ground. There were no ponds to freeze into a broad sheet of ice in late fall, no extra water available at pumps to cast out, bucket after bucket, onto a snow-packed field to make a rink in winter, nor any pools of meltwater to form a skating surface with a sharp frost in early spring. Still, we did manage to get some kind of rink, somehow, somewhere, some of the time.

In my ten years' attendance at our one-room country school, we had a skating rink for two of the winters. The schoolyard well was in the school's basement. It supplied the household needs of the teacher and his family, who lived in a teacherage nearby, so already was used to capacity. Yet one sports-minded teacher decided that with the well pumped empty each day—ensuring that his wife had some pails standing full in her kitchen—there might be enough water to make and flood a skating rink.

The water, of course, had to be carried up the stairs and out a side door, and this was no small feat, considering that most of us could not even carry a full bucket on a straightaway. And carrying only a half bucket would double the work time—we had only our fifteen-minute recesses and a noon hour each day. So two students gripped each bucket handle, trying to step in unison up the narrow stairs.

Then it was on to the growing patch of water-soaked snow, inner arms straining obliquely and outer arms held out at right angles in counterbalance. The water, sloshing to the rim, spilled on pantlegs (and froze), but most was delivered to one of the older students at rinkside, who swung out the pail's contents in a broad arc and packed down the mushy snow into a smooth surface.

Even with a dozen pairs of students carrying water, the bucket brigade moved slowly, despite our running back with the empty bucket for a refill in competition with other "drawers of water." Then we found a way to bypass the stairs. A basement window could be swung open and a bucket of water lifted to the ledge from inside by the heftiest boy in school, standing on a trestle. We bucket-brigaders remained outside to pick up our full pail at the window and return the empty pail there.

When the well went dry, we were through for the day, the last pail being brown with sand and not suitable for a skating rink. But the next day there would be more water, and the rink finally reached its desired size. After that, it was only a matter of flooding, and flooding again, once more by bucketfuls, to provide a permanent, hard, smooth surface. Thus, after several weeks, the rink was ready.

Just as we had made the rink in a democratic fashion, further democratic procedure was needed to decide how we would use it. Naturally we boys wanted to play hockey every day, but that left no skating time for the girls. With our teacher as consultant, we arrived at this compromise: Tuesday and Thursday would be skating days; Wednesday and Friday, hockey. Monday was for cleaning and re-flooding the surface. Often it snowed over the weekend, so on Monday we were also busy with homemade scrapers, shovels, and brooms. After a few snowfalls (and clearings), we had a nice snowbank around the rink in lieu of boards, so a hockey puck could thud into the snow instead of skimming far afield.

What a motley crowd we were on the ice, whether just skating or playing hockey. Some of us had no skates and went sliding about in our shoes. Most had skates of some kind—tube, blade, or bob—but usually they were hand-me-downs and ill fitting so that the youngest progressed across the ice in Mr. Winkle-like fashion, their ankles weak and balance unsure. I learned to skate on my cousin's bobskates, graduated to a pair of tube skates, then fell heir to my sister's blade skates. The soft leather of her skates provided no ankle support at all, and being several sizes too large, they flopped about on my feet—I wore down the inner edges of the soles by skating on them.

But we persisted, nearly freezing our feet every noon hour, then sitting at our desks in stocking feet with whitened, numbed toes, getting feeling back in them accompanied by itching and prickling—all this while trying to concentrate on arithmetic or social studies. Still, we never could have enough of skating. Since we did not have time to put on and take off skates—let alone do any skating—during the short recesses, we bargained with our teacher to shorten these to a five-minute stretch period and increase our noon hour by a whole twenty minutes. More chilblains!

A few years elapsed before another skating rink was possible. The water table had sunk so low that the basement well just could not supply enough water. But there was another well outside the schoolyard fence that a farmer used for livestock. One winter he announced that we could use the water from it: he had another source for his cows. It was an old well with a pulley and bucket.

Again, paired youngsters carried sloshing pails of water, and older students managed the pulley and the rinkside flooding. With the normal splashing that occurred at the well, its cribbing soon became coated with ice, thicker and thicker, until the opening for the descending bucket to plunge through grew too small. Then someone had to slash away the ice with a hatchet, holding up our brigade. But eventually we had a rink.

A third attempt, another year, was unsuccessful. By that time, though, the farmer's well had caved in, but another farmer half a mile away said we were welcome to use his if we could get the water to the schoolyard. Farm children are innovative and self-reliant when it comes to these things, and so we planned to haul the water by cistern using a horse and cutter, which many of us drove to school. Unfortunately, our noon hours were too short to get the job done. Even if two boys left immediately at twelve—they could eat their lunch later—they usually returned after the bell rang at one o'clock and sheepishly took their seats. The teacher never said anything—he admired our initiative—but at that pace we finally gave up the project and took to playing soccer in the snow.

Those students whose farmyards had wells with more than enough water were lucky. With a little industry, perhaps the help of an older brother, they could make their own private rink, however small. During one winter I spent a Sunday afternoon at the farmyard from which we had hauled water, skating circles on a postage-stamp rink. Skiing two miles cross-country in the freezing cold for a few hours of uninterrupted skating on a tiny rink was still a real privilege.

But for me the best rural skating rink of all was a frozen pond. This might be open gray ice in cold November days before the first snowfall, or dark ice swept clean of blanketing snows in midwinter, or a stretch of meltwater ice reflecting spring skies amid that season's dirty snowbanks. When late-fall rains or sudden spring thaws made such ice available, my cousin and I headed to the nearest pond, our skates dangling over our shoulders, a hockey stick in hand. If it was spring, we set out in early morning before the ice started to melt.

Often such ponds were fringed by willow clumps, and it was exciting to skate around them into corridors lined with branches and then burst out onto an open expanse of ice again, skate blades swishing rhythmically across the drumlike surface, the cool, invigorating air streaming by our faces. Before the morning or afternoon was over, a few other farm boys might be whirling over the ice, this time chasing an elusive hockey puck, cradling it alternately on either side of the stick in a mad dash to score a goal or set one up.

The great stickhandlers of olden-day hockey—Max Bentley, for example—are said to have learned their supreme skill on just such small prairie ponds, playing shinny amid a crowd of players—it was the only way to keep control of the puck, with so many sticks on the ice. I can easily believe it.

Much as I enjoyed the camaraderie of these rinks, my most memorable times were coming upon an outdoor pond toward evening when it was deserted. A moon might be rising over the treetops, making the ice appear all the darker, surrounded as it was by glistening snow. I could hear myself breathe (and see each puff of air I exhaled) in that silent dream world. Hunched on a snowbank, I laced up my skates, then took a few preliminary strides across the glassy surface. My skates rang in the clear air as I lengthened the sweep of each blade.

I was now an explorer in shadowed ghost lands as I swerved around willow clumps and through clutching branches. I felt akin to the protagonist in "The Skater and the Wolves," a story in our *Highroads* reader, where the skater eludes a pack of wolves that slips through the moonlit forest beside the stream on which he is skating. We had no wolves, but we had coyotes, and their wavering cry in sudden concert often broke the stillness—non-threatening, but giving an eerie sensation down the back of my neck.

Cold and moonlight and ringing blade on echoing ice, and now the true wilderness given voice in the coyotes' yelping: it was an ideal skating "arena." I felt like "the god of winged heel" in Charles G. D. Roberts's wonderful poem "The Skater," with "glittering steel" shoeing my "glad feet." So I coursed ahead in my solitary flight, and "the blood sang high in my eager brain."

Olden-Day Skiing

Today cross-country skiing makes us think of laminated fiberglass skis with wood cores, skillfully crafted and perhaps no more than three inches wide. The bindings accept only a specifically designed ski boot—preferably with a softly padded, high-cut upper portion to facilitate ankle movement, an acrylic lining inside for warmth, and a polyurethane outer layer for waterproofing. To think that the simple equipment we used sixty years ago would give way to such elaborate high-tech improvements!

My first pair of skis was homemade, constructed of fir (not the best choice, for it proved to be splintery). After one end of each board was sawn to a point, this tip was soaked for several hours in boiling water. It could then be bent upward while the rest of the ski was held in a vise. A stout wire was looped about the pointed end, secured farther down the ski, and twisted, to bring the tip up even more and prevent it from curving back while the wood slowly dried. My skis, by this means, were the deluxe model of homemade skis. (Some were only flat boards with pieces of bent tin nailed to the front to serve as tips.)

The harness was a single leather toe strap fastened down by passing under a notched, thin, foot-length board screwed firmly to the ski. This accommodated any kind of footwear, from moccasin to sturdy boot, for a person simply pushed his toe into the upright leather loop.

As a boy I wore "packfillers" throughout the day in winter. Rather formless in shape, these were one-piece footgear of molded black felt, nearly half an inch thick, reaching higher than the ankles and having metal eyelets and laces. So donning skis did not mean changing into other footwear first.

I did not use ski poles, although my sister used one sawed-off broom handle for extra support. When I skied cross-country to school, I needed my hands for clutching my lunch pail and books; ski poles would have made things cumbersome. (A backpack would have freed my hands, but I didn't think it was necessary.)

I also did a lot of skiing for pleasure. My ski trail started at our house and radiated in the direction, freshly made, in which I decided to ski. The skis when not in use were stuck into a snowdrift just outside the door or else into the snow banked against the house for insulation. I had merely to slip on an aviator cap and mackinaw (parkas were not yet available), mitts, and rubbers, and step out the door to begin the day's adventure.

Homemade skis were from four to five inches wide, necessary when the trail was really *cross-country*. Half the time a person was

skiing over stubble fields where breaking through the snow's thin crust was all too easy. At fence lines the wide skis proved extra reliable. Farmers did not use weed sprays, and fences tended to have an extensive growth of weeds and brush along them (which, incidentally, harbored considerable bird life in the summertime). When the fencerows filled up with snow in winter, it was often possible to ski over the top of a fence without breaking through. Where some strands of barbed wire still showed above the drifted snow, it was no trick to ski the front half of the ski under the wire, step out of the single-strap harness, and while still standing on the skis (so as not to break through the snow), crawl over or between the wires, slip back into the harness, and continue skiing—without having to stoop to unhitch or fasten the harness.

So cross-country skiing proceeded, alone on a random course, skiing out of the way to investigate a curious hummock of snow or stopping on a rise of land to let the eyes sweep along the circle of horizon. One was trying *not* to reach any specified destination, but letting the activity take care of itself. Often there were jackrabbit tracks to observe, like dice patterns in the snow, and following them might lead anywhere. Sometimes there were tracks to be deciphered—perhaps a meadow vole's scurrying prints, after it had burrowed upward to the surface from its grass-lined runway at ground level. Where the tracks suddenly stopped and a snowy owl's wing tips had brushed the snow—was this the survival of the fittest? And who had been the fittest in this drama—the hungry owl on silent wings or the frightened vole plunging down through white depths to safety?

A skier would almost certainly, somewhere along his course, flush up a covey of plump gray partridges feeding on weed stalks or perhaps nestling in a snowdrift. With a whirring clatter of wings and rapid cackling, the reddish brown birds would rocket away, low over the ground, giving life and color to an otherwise seemingly sterile landscape. More distant, the flock would take to gliding on stiffly arched wings, their cackling slowing down and ceasing altogether, as they streamed over a hill and out of sight.

The best time for skiing was in February or March, when we had already had a number of blizzards. The surfaces were not only hard but were sculpted and honed by the wind into a variety of reliefs: ribbed slopes, undulating plains, and swerving dunes. Each type of snow cover heightened the experience—for me an indulging of a kinesthetic sense, feeling muscles work in legs and feet as I adjusted my pace for each terrain, and experiencing the world in a simple primitive fashion. But the subtle tints of the many-textured snow were my chief interest and all the more prevalent in the lingering light of the lengthening days of late winter.

As the sun sank toward the western skyline, the snow became blue and deeper blue, reflecting the darkening sky high above, yet complementing the dusky orange of sunset sky along the horizon. Some slopes might show a pinkish cast for a brief interval in the changing light, then give way to indigo and violet, always maintaining some blueness even by starlight in later evening.

Other winter scenes were also part of my boyhood skiing expeditions. I liked an overcast sky when the outdoor world was an unremitting gray—leaden sky, leafless trees, and shadowed snow. One winter, I remember, had a lot of clouded (and snow-filled) days, and I was taking a high-school grade by correspondence lessons on the farm, studying at our dining-room table.

At the end of the school day I set off by ski to a hay meadow in the corner of the farm. There the heavy snowfalls and accompanying storms had completely covered several willow clumps that stood on a slight rise beside a small pond. This was my "downhill" ski run, and I made the most of it, skiing off the willow bushes and gliding across the pond over and over.

Although real hills for skiing purposes were lacking, there actually was a very good substitute—straw stacks from fall threshing. Whenever I was cross-country skiing and came to one, I could not resist climbing up with my skis and coasting down.

Usually my first attempt was done sitting on the skis in toboggan fashion to gain a better idea of the slope and its foibles while making a proper ski trail. There might be tufts of straw that could hook a ski and send it skedaddling from underneath me so that the downward slide would end on a single ski. A little repair work to the run would take care of the problem. Still, the first attempt at standing upright on the skis always gave a few anxious moments.

Perhaps my fondest memories occurred one winter when we had a straw stack on a field south of our yard. After supper when chores were done and a bright full moon shone down on a glistening world, I skied out to my downhill straw-stack run. Poised at the top, I looked over the silent landscape, the bright snow reflecting back the yellow moonlight, the frosty air much colder at nighttime.

Then down the stack I sailed in my swishing headlong flight, the frosty wind streaming by. Coming to a gradual stop some distance away, I paused momentarily, my breath once more visible before my face as I breathed deeply again. Stepping out a pattern like spokes in a wheel, I turned with my skis back to the straw stack and, once there, scrambled up it to repeat the performance—many times.

The moon moved in space, ever higher, turning the winter world to silver, and one active farm boy found waiting wings to sail down once more. The temperature grew a few degrees colder; the skis crunched through the snow more loudly in the night air.

Finally it was time to ski home. The light from a coal-oil lamp shone from the windows, and curling smoke rose from the chimney. It was good to burst into the warm house and the fellowship there after the invigorating activity of the outdoors, knowing that my homemade skis were just outside, ready to be used again on some other carefree cross-country jaunt.

Tires and Stilts

"Small things amuse small minds," or so it is said condescendingly. But such was happily the case sixty years ago. Some simple item could help us to while away our free time for days on end, for an entire summer in fact, and even for several summers in succession. Take tires and stilts, for instance. Both gave some sense of adulthood to a child, and that was probably part of their lingering appeal.

With tires it was just a matter of finding an old discarded one and rolling it along beside you as you ran in play about the farmyard or scurried along a trail to visit at a neighboring farm, where the children were also rolling tires about. Each child seemed to be driving his own vehicle, in control of it, like a grown-up.

These "vehicles" were not hard to come by. During the Great Depression many farmers could not afford to drive cars, so converted Model T chassis into Bennett wagons, but tires wore out on wagons, too. Even where new tires could not be afforded for the wagon (our wagon rattled along on the rims), the discarded tires were still there to be rolled along by eager children.

What was the object of the activity, you might ask. There was no real object, and that was the beauty of it. You were simply rolling a tire.

It was a kind of "companion" that went where you went, like the child's shadow in Robert Louis Stevenson's poem, and you rolled it along by stroking it forward with a free hand. When you went inside the house, you could "park" it by the door, leaning it against the wall, ready for use as soon as you returned outdoors.

Of course, you could make up competitions with yourself: trying to roll the tire all the way to your neighbor's yard, a half-mile distant, without it once going out of control. This it might easily do by running off the trail or turning crosswise in a sandy area. (Remember that the tire would probably be more than waist-high to the boy rolling it along.)

Country roads were two parallel paths with grass between them—the wheel tracks of wagon traffic—and a small boy had difficulty keeping a tire from catching on the edge of the sod. Then it would begin to wobble, and although some decisive slaps or thrusts might straighten its course, most times it would start flopping from side to side, then lean one way, more and more, while still slowly turning, finally inscribing a circle on the ground just before falling flat.

On one occasion I recall returning with my tire from my grandmother's home a mile away when I became aware of a horse and buggy coming up behind me. I immediately knew that here was a neighbor about to make a call on my parents. For some reason I was determined that he should not pass me and my tire—so I speeded up.

I had a good head start, but I also had a good run ahead of me. No time to have my tire swiveling off-course now on the varied terrain! Going down a hill was all right, for I had to run at my utmost then anyway just to keep up with my rolling tire. But now I found I had to run at a good clip going up the next hill to maintain my lead on the buggy, panting hard and slapping away at the tire.

I persevered, however, and with the sound of a horse's hoofs behind me, probably set some kind of record for tire-rolling that day in the small-boy classification.

There was one other thing we sometimes did as a childhood amusement with rolling tires, especially a large tire, but it was never something we persisted at. The effect was too dizzying. One of us would sit hunched up within the tire, as if we were the wheel it was fitted on, while someone else rolled it along. And so we made a vertical merry-go-round exclusively for one person, but we never felt very merry after the ride. The tire had been driving us, and we were no longer in control.

Now with stilts, that other simple amusement, there was again a feeling of being in charge of our own "vehicle," as we went high-stepping about the yard. And there was another attraction to this form of locomotion. We had suddenly risen to the height of adults, seeing the world from a different level, a view from their prospect.

Unlike rolling tires, however, stilt-walking required a short period of practice before one became adept at it. A novice learned how most easily by mounting the stilts while they were leaning against a wall. With his own back to the wall (for physical *and* moral support) and hands grasping the stilts firmly halfway down, while elbows pressed the top ends firmly against his sides, he pushed off with one or two faltering steps.

Keeping in balance was the trick, and spills could be avoided if he knew enough to step to the ground with one foot when things began to waver. Otherwise down would come stilts, stilt-walker, and all.

After a few trials, success was assured. Because a skill was developed, there was a great sense of accomplishment felt by a young child, and for a time stilt-walking became a passion.

Again, there was no real object to walking with them as in some regular games—no points to make or runs or goals to score. No, they were just there for one to stroll about the yard, enjoying the view. Like the tire, they could be left at the door, ready at hand when one wanted them.

Soon a person learned to stand more or less motionless on the stilts as well as to walk extended distances. Did his mother want some vegetables from the garden to cook for dinner? No problem—stilts carried him down to the garden and back and made work into playtime.

Later, when I was taking high school, I was introduced to Euclid's formal geometry and its two basic figures, the straight line and the circle. I could not help but think that they were like the stilts and tires of my earlier childhood, made abstract, those simple times that had provided so much innocent pleasure.

Their appeal still lingered, now not because of a feeling they gave of driving a vehicle like an adult, or seeing the world from his higher elevated viewpoint, but of their seeming involvement with Euclid's so different theoretical world of plane logic—parallel and intersecting lines and enclosing circles. I wondered whether this sage and venerable Greek mathematician of ancient times had ever played with some kind of stilts and tires when he was a child.

The Old Farm Organ

My mother's first Christmas gift from Dad was a pedal or pump organ. It was 1918 and our house was still a fourteen-by-twenty-foot uninsulated shack.

The new organ was a six-octave "Eaton" brand, ordered of course from the T. Eaton Company of Winnipeg. It arrived at the railway station in Rosthern and was then hauled home by bobsleigh. Experiencing first the winter's sharp cold during transportation, the organ next encountered the fierce heat of the shack's one stove trying to ward off icy drafts in the roughly built house.

My parents were not going to sink down under harsh pioneer times, but instead "get some color and music out of life." I am thinking here of a line from Robert Frost's poem "The Investment." Buying an organ, even if one could barely afford it, was a much-needed investment then.

Mother had begun to play an organ when she was seven. At that time her mother had received an organ from *her* husband as part of the furnishings of their new frame house. Up to then the family had lived in a sod-roofed hut, their first home on emigrating from Minnesota in 1899—the year of my mother's birth. My grandmother played mostly hymns from notes that to her were the numbers one to seven (an octave's range) rather than the letters of the alphabet.

Mother started to pick out tunes by ear despite Grandmother's comment that her fingers were too short to play. Mother only tried the harder. And she taught herself to play from notes as well; for her, since she learned this in school, they were *do, re, mi*'s and not numbers.

Learning this kind of musical notation was really an advantage, for then she could play *do, re, mi*'s anywhere on the scale to suit the singing voices of the neighborhood girls who crowded about the organ for an old-fashioned songfest—or the young men who accompanied her on violin. All the young men in her district, she recalled, could play violin, just as her father did.

With her flair for playing by ear, Mother would entertain herself (and others), pumping the organ with her feet and playing for hours. Stephen Foster melodies were particular favorites. When she was not playing, tunes danced in her head. Music was a big part of her life.

One day when she was twelve, her family drove to Fish Creek on the South Saskatchewan River for a picnic. While stopping at the store run by Joseph and Angeline Branconnier, she heard someone at another organ playing "Silver Threads Among the Gold," a new tune for Mother. My, she was taken by the melody. It was the highlight of the excursion.

She started saving her pennies so she could order the sheet music. When it came, she learned the song, rather difficult to play for a young girl who had never had any lessons. Her success encouraged her to order the sheet music for a few other songs whose titles intrigued her: "Moon Winks," "Just A-Wearyin' for You," and "Sailor's Hornpipe."

Now, in 1918, she was to get her very own organ, and she could hardly wait. It was ordered well ahead of Christmas, almost two months in advance, for it was still wartime and things could be delayed. The war ended in mid-November, but delays continued. The organ did not come—and did not come. When only a few days remained till Christmas, she began checking at the station. It just had to come, but it just did not.

So the winter wore on, into the new year and eventually into February. Mother still called at the station occasionally, but, no, nothing was there. What could have happened? Finally, in early March, the much-awaited Christmas gift arrived. There was great excitement in getting it home and uncrated.

There it stood, rather imposing, for it was an "upright," like modern-day pianos, and not the lower model that Mother knew from her childhood. It was a little disappointing, too, in its staid blackish appearance—not much "color" to "get out of life" from that, so different from the warm brown finish of her mother's organ. As for the "music" component (Frost's poem again), my mother's sensitive ear told her that it lacked the rich tone of the organ known from childhood. Oh well, such disappointments were short-lived. Wartime delays and workmanship would not faze her. Here was a new organ, and she was eager to play it. The little shack resounded with melody that evening—several hours of it.

Over the next years, Mother (playing) and Dad (listening) got a lot of music out of their lives and even some color: as the organ's black paint wore thin in places, a reddish undertone showed through (as did the seams of what was a veneer finish, not solid wood). Mother continued playing, despite her many chores, inside and out; her fingers turned out to be extremely nimble on the keyboard. Ours was a house of music.

As we children came along, we caught some of her enthusiasm. My sister, Elsie, sang at the organ while chording in accompaniment, and my older brother, Ernie, worked at selected hit-parade tunes. My next brother Ted really had Mother's flair for music, but in a more modern style, playing by ear and improvising for hours. (It was years later, when I heard the music score from the movie *The Sting*, that I realized what my mother had been playing, true to her era, was ragtime.)

At first I was most interested in the organ's twelve stops that could be pushed in and pulled out. What exotic labels they bore (and in fancy script), names like "Diapason," "Dulciana," and

"Vox Humana." When I learned to chord, I did so on the black keys, for with my small hands they were the easiest to play. Consequently I played in the key of F sharp (six sharps!), my sister showing me its four basic chords. And the first song I learned to chord to was a Second World War hit—"One Dozen Roses." In learning to play a guitar much later, I transposed my fingering there to the organ so that I could chord in a more sophisticated fashion—with minors, diminished sevenths, and so on.

After Mother became a widow in 1950 and moved to Saskatoon, she would play her organ only when she returned to the farm in the summer, something she did for the next two decades. By 1970 she was completely retired to Rosthern, but there was no room for the organ in her little house, so it remained on the farm, only played during some short visits there when I was around for holidays.

Then in 1981 she learned of "apartment" pianos from a sister-in-law, little pianos of just five octaves. Surely she could make room for one in her house. I encouraged her to get one, a Mason and Risch "Cameo" model.

It arrived on her eighty-second birthday that year. She was so

overjoyed with it she could hardly play. But before long, waltzes, schottisches, and the difficult "Sailor's Hornpipe" were resounding in her living room. It seemed as if she were a young girl again.

Over the next weeks she would awake at night with an old fiddle tune thrumming in her brain, a tune that one of the bundle pitchers on her father's threshing crew had played after a day's work. Quickly she would get pencil and paper to write down the melody in *do, re, mi*'s in order to play it next day as she once had on the organ. Such recall happened several times, enabling her to musically relive the past.

When I suggested she try some songs from the era in which I grew up, the 1940s, she obliged with her usual enthusiasm. These were reminders of days when we were all on the farm, around the organ—the "good old days," she called them. She particularly liked Rogers and Hammerstein's "It Might As Well Be Spring" and took extra pains to work out a fine arrangement of it, later playing it for different friends in town—and, sometimes, just for herself on the Eaton organ at the farm.

That organ, arriving late for Christmas 1918, thus continued to give "color and music" to her life seven decades later. Oh, the memories in old melodies, the good times and troubles too— "when the organ played at twilight the song[s] that reached my heart" (yet another well-known refrain of those days).

$\mathcal{L}$*amps*

In the year I was born, 1933, the popular song "When It's Lamp Lightin' Time in the Valley" began: "There's a lamp shinin' bright in a cabin, / In the window it's shinin' for me." I have always had an affection for lamps, particularly the coal-oil lamps used in the prairie farm homes of my boyhood. There were also mantle lamps, which gave a brighter light and, because of the air pressure inside, gave off an accompanying hiss. Often while doing chores outside, I saw our kitchen lamp through the window, its warm light bespeaking the closeness and security awaiting us indoors at the end of day.

Our kitchen lamp was the one my father bought when he began farming on his own in 1915, a handsome but simple coal-oil lamp to light his bachelor's shack; now some ninety years old, it stands in a place of honor in our living room. Made of clear glass, it has a circular foot about five inches across, a stem just long enough to permit a firm grasp with one hand, and a small ribbed oval bowl for kerosene. The bowl is fitted on top with an external threaded brass collar with a basal flange. (Later lamps did not have the flange, and still later ones had the collar fitted within the glass.)

The basic lamp stands nine inches high. Then there is the metal burner, which screws into the collar and holds (and turns up) the cotton wick, and, within its four clips, supports the glass chimney. The original chimney was made of very thin glass with a flared-out top and a crinkled edging, crimped while the glass was still soft. (Other later chimneys—those not having a straight cylindrical top—had a flared crinkled edge formed in a mold.)

The neat lamp held but two cups of kerosene, and this fact became significant. For when Dad married Mother, times were poor; they agreed that one filling of the lamp should last two nights. Thus in the short days of winter, the long snow-blue twilight became even darker before the lamp was lit. And then when the lamp was half-empty, or empty altogether, it was automatically bedtime. No clock was needed.

By the time I was born, they had bought a second lamp with a bigger bowl. It was just as well, for an addition had been built onto the shack and more than one room had to be lit. A decade later, at my parents' silver wedding anniversary in 1943, they received a gift of one dollar from one of Dad's sisters with which they bought another coal-oil lamp—the burner and chimney were extra. This was the largest and most colorful of our lamps. It had a blue foot and stem and a white bowl encircled with a red floral design. Dad's original lamp could now be put aside as a stand-by—the others did not need filling so often.

Sometime in the mid-1940s we bought the first of two mantle lamps. It was of all-iron construction, painted cream (some models had a nickeled base). The base itself held the fuel, and it was always filled outdoors, even on the coldest winter day, because the fuel was gasoline. When the lamp was taken inside again, we used a small hand pump to build up pressure inside the tank. (Our second lamp had a built-in pump.) Next we held a burning match to heat the "generator" and ignite the mantles, then opened the valve (and *never* in reverse order, for safety reasons). There was a slight *poof*, and the mantles glowed a bright yellowish white, giving excellent illumination. The generator could be turned to keep the jet from plugging.

The mantles were a marvel to my boyish mind. Made of cloth to start with, a pair was tied onto the lamp, then set aflame. All that remained were two slack mantles of ash. Yet under the pressure of the lighted gasoline vapor, they filled out and remained suspended for weeks and months—turning white hot with each evening's lighting and white cold when not in use during the day. So long as the lamp was not jarred, the mantles stayed intact. The greatest hazard came from flies bumping into them when they were unlit in summertime.

Years later, when I was teaching in a country school and living in a teacherage, I sometimes walked back to school in the evening to finish up my work, carrying a lighted lamp with its unprotected mantles. Even on nights when the temperature was near 40 degrees below, no harm was done. To carry the lamp, I gripped it by its stem/handle just below the burning mantles and made very sure not to stumble along the snowy pathway.

There was a long upright rod on top with a loop at the end for hanging the lamp from a hook in the ceiling. Two lamps hanging in a classroom during an evening Christmas concert provided ample light for the whole performance. The only problem was the lessening pressure in the lamps as the evening wore on: the light would grow dimmer. Then someone—usually one of the trustees—would have to unhook each lamp and pump it up again.

At home our mantle lamp either stood on the table or hung above it. So that someone getting up from the table would not inadvertently knock it off its hook, we used a closed hook bent open sideways. The lamp's looped end would have to be turned in order to get it onto the hook, and it could never be bumped off however much we might bump our heads on it.

At a neighbor's home, however, such a lamp, burning, was knocked off the hook above us while we were all sitting at the supper table. As the lamp plunged downward, and before anyone could say anything, in a pure reflex action my small hand shot out and caught it—luckily around the handle and not the burning mantles. No harm was done and a possibly serious accident was prevented. Needless to say, I was a hero for the next few minutes until we fell back to our eating.

Mother, when she returned to the farm each summer after my father died, did not want to fuss with mantles and pressure pumps and dangerous gasoline, so she went back to using the three coal-oil lamps. She had been young when she first used them, and it made her feel young to use them again. There was a pride in cleaning them each day and tending them each evening.

To facilitate filling lamps with kerosene, she poured the fuel from its outdoor galvanized container into an old granite pitcher. Then she could unscrew a burner and with one hand tilt it to one side so that its dripping wick remained in the bowl, leaving the other hand free to empty the pitcher into the lamp. With the burner screwed tight once more, she turned up the wick and trimmed off the burned end.

The chimney needed special attention. With a bit of crumpled newspaper, she squeezed her hand into the larger end and polished it clean of any accumulated smoke from the previous night's burning. (It was a point of personal satisfaction for a farm wife to have a hand small and flexible enough to go into a lamp chimney.) Finally the whole exterior of the lamp was given a polishing with the same bit of newspaper, and she would set it on a shelf with the others beside the kitchen range till they needed to be lit.

At nightfall this ritual proceeded: a match stroked across the top of the range, a small flare of light held steadily between thumb and forefinger and applied to the lamp's wick with the chimney raised (a faint kerosene smell greeting the nostrils), followed by the enveloping glow as the chimney came down—the house's interior was painted in ruddy tones again. It was good to be in the old familiar surroundings.

Meanwhile, a crackling fire in the stove took away the evening's chill, and the kettle, freshly filled, steamed away. At bedtime she might turn down the wick to leave a dim, friendly light throughout the house, or with her hand at the back edge of the chimney, direct a quick puff of air toward the flame and blow it out.

With electrification, other farms had no need for this primitive form of light. Only Mother, it seemed, still experienced the joy and ritual of a daily direct involvement with lighting a home. At this time I began to collect coal-oil lamps at farm auctions. Now I, too, could indulge an ongoing affection for the old-fashioned lamps, in the few I bought, cleaned, and restored.

They had such a variety of interesting shapes and colors. The oldest had a wrought-iron foot with a lovely curved white-glass bowl covered with scrollwork. Another of similar base had a huge, bulging, clear-glass bowl. Then there were the all-glass lamps, clear but delicately tinted—blue, rose, or green. And the rich design: they were basically circular or square or hexagonal, or a mix of all of these, some with added rims and diamond-shaped facets.

It was a joy for me to light my old lamps, just as it was for Mother. In a sense we were both "The Old Lamp-Lighter" (another popular song, from 1946). Like him, we lovingly lit the lamps each evening, "ma[king] the night a little brighter." We could both say with Canadian poet Kathleen Davidson, in her beautiful poem "Lamps"—

O I am all for little lamps
When the shadows loom ...

Adventures in Reading

In *So Long to Learn*, British poet John Masefield writes of his boyhood reading and of a "fastness" or hiding place in his home where he indulged in this pastime. It was under a bed with side valances reaching the floor, a place where he could lie undiscovered and, with adequate light from a bedroom window, pore over his book. I recall in my own boyhood a time when, unbeknown to my parents, I was safely out of sight, under the blankets on my bed, reading the last few pages of an exciting adventure story by flashlight. It was a book I could not put down even though the hour was considerably past my normal bedtime.

Reading was ever a delight to me, despite the many interesting things to do growing up on a farm. Books provided passage to other realms, new worlds to be lived in imaginatively, stretching one's mind and swelling one's heart. Our elementary-school *Highroads to Reading* texts earnestly reinforced this fact.

In grade two, for example, a quatrain spoke of a book as a treasure chest "packed to the top with the best / That this fine world can hold." In grade three another poem pictured a book as a "white-sailed ship" bearing us "To lands of flower, and lands of snow, / Bright shore and lonely bay." In the same reader Robert Louis Stevenson wrote of "The Land of Story-Books" in which he lived as a boy. Whatever the world entered, affirmed a poem from our grade-six reader, it was a private kingdom, an "inglenook" (akin to Masefield's "fastness"). With this kind of corroboration of the joys of reading, it is little wonder that many of my memorable reading adventures were associated with my school days. The readers had excerpts from classic books, with author and title listed, and these names remained with me so that when I came across the complete work, sometimes in much later years, I could relive, and extend, my earlier boyhood exhilaration from the first brief reading.

Thus "Rip Van Winkle" led me to read all of Washington Irving's *Sketchbook*; "Cuff's Fight with Dobbin," Thackeray's *Vanity Fair*; "Escape from the Press Gang," Hardy's *The Trumpet Major*; and "Dotheboys Hall," Dickens's *Nicholas Nickleby*. Similarly, other pieces prompted me eventually to read Charles Kingsley's *Hereward the Wake* and Charles G. D. Roberts's *Around the Camp-Fire*. All were great books, and I read some of them more than once.

At times the excerpt seemed complete and sufficient in itself. I recall listening in on a story being studied by the grade eight class, "Grim Shadows Lie on the Water," by nature photographer-writer Cherry Kearton, taken from his book *The Animals Came To Drink*. It featured a fearsome combat between two giant crocodiles in the African wilds.

To me, in grade one, it was a perfectly enthralling story, and in grade two, I listened again with rapt eagerness, as I would in grades three, four, and five. By grade six I knew I had only two more years to wait to read it for myself, and in grade seven I was already basking in my soon-to-be unique reading adventure.

The old rural schools, with their multi-graded crowding, had a natural enrichment program that modern urban classrooms, with all their technical expertise and facilities, cannot duplicate. For, finally, I was in grade eight, and it was *my* reader that had the wonderfully titled "Grim Shadows Lie on the Water," mine to read and study and savor. What a thrill! Realization was just as sweet as anticipation.

Although we had splendid readers, our school library was

quite slim. Still, we had the opportunity to read a few key books—and to re-read them, which, after all, is one of the principal joys of this reading adventure. I particularly liked *Lives of the Hunted* by Ernest Thompson Seton, who captured in his writing the feeling of wilderness. His descriptions were superb: "So, in this land of long, long winter night where Nature stints her joys of six hard months, … the spring is glorious compensation for the past. Six months arrears of joy are paid in one vast lavish outpour." Krag, the Kootenay Ram, was one of the *Hunted* in this wilderness, and the account of his travails remained gripping each time I read it.

The lives of legendary heroes were great reading fare, too. Both *The Merry Adventures of Robin Hood* by Howard Pyle and any compilation of the tales of King Arthur and his Knights of the Round Table were exciting stuff. We felt an empathy with Robin Hood's sense of fair play and good fellowship and were heroically stirred by Arthur and Lancelot's code of chivalry. With either story we could follow, in a sense, the motto of practical education proclaimed by Squeers of Dotheboys Hall: "When a boy knows this [lesson] out of book, he goes and does it."

For us a poplar bluff on the schoolyard could well be Sherwood Forest, for its branches enabled us to build a bower, and its saplings provided us with bows and quarterstaves. It could also be an enchanted forest for knights slaying dragons or questing heroic adventures. The medieval language of these books caught our fancies, and our speech became larded with "prithee" and "thou" and "my liege," also "have at thee, varlet!"

Books of real live heroes fascinated me as well, especially *The Story of Abraham Lincoln* by Mary A. Hamilton. A small bluish gray volume in the Thomas Nelson and Sons "Children's Heroes Series," its subject was an apt role model—diligent, honest, and visionary. Certain details in Lincoln's life not only caught my interest then but still strike me as significant: he had only a few books to read in his boyhood, but he read them again and again until he knew everything in them; clerking in a store as a young man, he once walked several miles out of his way to repay a customer the six and a quarter cents that he had unknowingly shortchanged her; and later, as president, he maintained his faith in common people, saying that God seemed to prefer them for He made so many of them.

Our school library also had two books about ordinary students. One, Thomas Hughes's *Tom Brown's School Days*, we read because its world was *not* ours—that of a boy at a private school with a dormitory. The games, cricket and rugby, were foreign to us; the staff, headmaster and praepostor, unfamiliar; the grades, lower fourth form and so on, quite strange. And what was study fagging? But we enjoyed the exoticism of it and appreciated the school spirit that, apparently, existed among pupils everywhere.

The other book, Gene Stratton-Porter's *The Girl of the Limber-lost*, we read because its incidents echoed those of our school and neighborhood. The young girl, Elnora Comstalk, starting high school in a nearby town, could have foreshadowed any one of us a few years hence, she ill at ease in strange surroundings and feeling very countrified when her name was pronounced "cornstalk." Most of us would have neither the nerve nor the money to go on with our education in town or would at least delay doing so by taking a few years of high school by correspondence courses first. Those who did persist, as a few of our older brothers and sisters had done, would indeed need to

show Elnora's pluck and self-reliance.

Another school library book, which I never did finish reading, was Victor Hugo's *Toilers of the Sea*. One of the newer books in school, its fine dust jacket pictured a swimmer in the ocean depths with an octopus's tentacle curled about his ankle. My deskmate, a grade below me, would read the book next year but was anxious to learn the fate of the swimmer.

Well, the story was rather involved, and I read, as time allowed, for several weeks.

"Is the man caught by the octopus yet?" my deskmate kept asking.

"No," I answered him, "not yet."

Finally, the octopus had grasped the poor man just at a chapter's end. "Yep, he's got him," I whispered to my fellow student. We were both excited now.

The next time I picked up the book, I had not read far when my deskmate nudged me with his elbow. "What happened?" he wanted to know.

"I don't know," was all I could reply. "The story's now shifted to something else."

So I continued reading, and my deskmate continued nudging me in the ribs. But I could never satisfy his curiosity, nor my own. The story seemed to advance the plot elsewhere, while our swimmer struggled for his life. Then it was June, our school year drew to its close, and I had to give up the book.

When fall came, I had new studies and new interests and other books to read—and my deskmate had moved with his family to South America! *Toilers of the Sea* was somehow put aside, the swimmer still grappling with his foe. At times I wonder what happened still, more than fifty years later. If I ever come across the book, I plan to finish it and find out.

Since our library had so few books, our teachers sometimes loaned us their own. In grade five I was loaned George Eliot's *The Mill on the Floss,* for the teacher thought I might like its complex weave of events in the lives of Maggie and Tom Tulliver and their parents. I do not recall my initial reaction to this Victorian book, but I am happy to have been introduced to it back then, for I have re-read it as an adult and it ranks among my favorite novels.

I had three other sources for borrowing books in my child-hood. My town cousins one winter lent me their three-volume set of *Heidi*. That I had just studied Switzerland in grade-three social studies gave impetus to my wishing to read it. Then an onset of flu gave me the opportunity to stay home and read about the small girl skipping through alpine meadows amid pas-turing goats and sleeping in a "loft" in her grandfather's hut—I liked this last notion.

I liked even more to read about the goatherd Peter, for his life reminded me of stories my father told of his boyhood herd-ing cows. The two sequels, detailing Heidi's later life (written by Charles Tritten, the translator of Johanna Spyri's original book), were of equal interest because Peter became a painter, and I was interested in painting. By the time I returned the books a month later, I had read not only all three but also each of the sequels twice.

One of my aunts was another source of books. She had her own riding horse and liked to read Zane Grey novels and other westerns. I remember borrowing Will James's *Smoky*, a loping-along cowboy yarn about a memorable one-man horse, all told in colorful western lingo. (As a boy, I liked to use terms such as "knowed" and "sashayed" as much as the Arthurian "certes" and "nay.")

Memorable, too, was another of my aunt's books, a hold-over from her own school days: *The Coral Island* by R. M. Ballantyne. This tale of Ralph Rover, Jack, and Peterkin (three boys ship-wrecked on their own Pacific island) was high adventure, what with a shark circling the log the three chums paddle offshore; the hideaway cave approached through an under-water entrance; the myriad resources of breadfruit, candlenut, and banyan trees; and the penguins—I was fascinated by the penguins. Unfortunately, for me, the book tailed off halfway through, once other characters reached the island.

My aunt also owned several Ralph Connor novels. I particularly liked *The Runner*, set during the 1812 War and detailing the battles at Queenston Heights, where General Isaac Brock lost his life, and at Lundy's Lane, the book's climax. Already familiar with the names, from singing "The Maple Leaf Forever" at school, I could vividly envision the unfolding dramatic events while reading the tale. The title character, a youth called René LaFlamme, was all a hero should be, and I liked the name of his horse, Gypsy, which he shortened to Gyp, the name of our farm dog.

The third source of books was a makeshift library in town. After my older brother had entered high school there (shades of Elnora Comstalk a.k.a. Cornstalk), he informed me that a few shelves of books in one of the classrooms were being made available for out-of-town borrowers, with an attendant on hand on Friday evenings. So I made my first venture into a real "library," gravitating to the shelf of westerns. The attendant lady pointed out there were other books to read, popular "children's" books that had lately been made into movies.

Thus, I read Eric Knight's *Lassie Come Home* and Mary O'Hara's *My Friend Flicka* and *Thunderhead*. At the time I liked *Thunderhead* best, with its tale of a young boy setting out alone to capture a magnificently named free-ranging horse.

With all my "travels" in reading, a final satisfying adventure needed to be fulfilled—owning books, a shelf or two of them, their multi-colored backs inviting my gaze. "Here stand my books, line upon line," I, with anthologist Andrew Lang, hoped to say with some pride. And so I built up a "library," first with gifts, later with my own purchases.

Christmas often brought me a present that I might read in its entirety on that very day before placing it on my bookshelf. *Canoe Mates in Canada* by St. George Rathborne was one such gift, a story of fur-trading days set in our neck of the woods and interesting on that account alone. It was subtitled *Afloat on the Saskatchewan*, after the river that flowed just a few miles away. Years later I wrote a lengthy history of the same era along the Saskatchewan River, and Rathborne's book helped to spark my initial interest in the subject.

Filling my shelf quickly was a special kind of children's book popular in my boyhood, the "Better Little Book," a fat volume of more than four hundred pages, measuring only three-and-a-half by four-and-a-half inches. Since it cost but fifteen cents (later twenty-five), a small investment soon had a half-dozen or so books "line upon line" along my shelf. Many retold the adventures of comic-strip characters—every other page was a picture—but some featured unknown personalities. I still remember *The Desert Eagle and the Hidden Fortress* and *Skeezix: On His Own in the Big City*.

Pinocchio I owned, both as a Better Little Book and a full-edition dust-jacketed clothbound volume. Carlo Collodi's wonderful sad tale of a wooden puppet come to life certainly stirred my imagination—my mother said not to read it all at once if I found it too moving. I remember I was quite small at the time, it being perhaps the first book I owned. Over the years I read it many times, and I still own it, in more-or-less new condition.

I kept adding books to my shelves. When our household received a new Eaton's catalog, I pored over the book page. There they were: dozens of books costing only twenty-nine or thirty-five cents—often twenty-nine or thirty-five cents more than I had. How their titles intrigued me! I looked at them longingly, wondering what "lands of flower, and lands of snow, / Bright shore and lonely bay" they would point to. Maybe another Christmas would bring an answer about one of them.

My budding library also had reference books, which I treasured. My parents went to Saskatoon one summer, and my mother brought back a slim thirty-page volume about the earth in the solar system, part of a set of a child's *Book of Knowledge*. Over the next few years she bought me three more books in the series—on plants, animals, and familiar things. In the meantime I had acquired three other reference books, all tiny in size: *Airplanes of the U.S.A.*, *The Red Book of Dogs*, and *How To Be a Good Swimmer*.

One of my mother's favorite childhood books was *Swiss Family Robinson*. She liked it well enough to name one of my brothers for a character in it. So when I had saved up thirty-five cents, I ordered the book from Eaton's.

Alas, when the order came, the book sent was Daniel Defoe's *Robinson Crusoe*. I was disappointed (I suppose Mother was, too), but I proceeded to read it anyway. Say, this was exciting stuff, once I got past all the details of Crusoe's early life. Here was a man completely alone, making his way in nature not through sheer genius or the discovery of fabulous resources but by a plodding businesslike acceptance of his circumstances and making the best of them.

Yet, to me, there were elements of romance as well—sleeping in a tree the first night on his island, finding a cave for his quarters, making his clothes from the skins of wild goats, keeping a calendar by cutting notches in a board. How fortunate I was to have been sent this sterling book, the ultimate saga of survival: universal man confronting the elements. For the next decade I read it every year. (I later started reading *Swiss Family Robinson* but gave it up when the events, supposedly lifelike, became too incredible.)

Another book I read not only every year but at a specific time. This was during the latter days of February when the winter already seemed long and the blue twilights extended further into the night, making one look for spring and the warm, carefree days of summer. Then I reached for *Huckleberry Finn* and, snuggled up beside our needfully glowing living-room heater, began reading: "You don't know about me, without you have read a book by the name of 'The Adventures of Tom Sawyer,' but that ain't no matter." That fact was truly not of any matter, for I had not read *Tom Sawyer* and did not need to to enjoy what became my favorite book.

How I came to own *Huckleberry Finn* is a story in itself. I did not buy it, nor was it exactly a gift. A city aunt and uncle, on moving to another province, sent us a box of discarded things we might make use of. Among them was a tattered set of *The Book of Knowledge* (the adult edition, which I more or less read through—that was good reading for a growing boy who liked to know about things), and an even more tattered *Huckleberry Finn*. This was the real prize.

Just as I had enjoyed *Canoe Mates in Canada* or *Afloat on the Saskatchewan*, so I now became absorbed in Mark Twain's book of "afloat on the Mississippi." I, too, wanted to float down a river, imbibing the sights and sounds, and now, until such time became reality, I could do it vicariously through Huck.

Through him I could sense the greatness of his river and, consequently, of my own, six miles away. It was, as he says, "awful still and grand," and so, I felt, was mine, for I had camped on its banks and known its awe-inspiring presence in early mornings, with mists rising from its waters, and in late evenings, with its now glassy surface holding the day's remaining light when all else had succumbed to darkness. It was like a living thing, rolling along, a central force affecting the lives of people along its shores—just as I came to realize that Huck's Mississippi was a central force or character in Twain's book, bringing Huck into contact with a broad mix of humanity as it flowed along, yet being itself unaffected.

What appealed to me particularly on each re-reading was Huck's closeness to the river and his hymn of praise in describing its beauty each morning and his joy in living on it then: "and next you've got the full day, and everything smiling in the sun, and the song-birds just going it! ... [A]fterwards we would watch the lonesomeness of the river, and kind of lazy along .... It's lovely to live on a raft."

Huck's raft was like the poet's "white-sailed ship" described in my grade-three reader. It, of my boyhood adventures in reading, was the greatest of "chariot[s] / That bear ... a human soul" so many "leagues away," as Emily Dickinson says in her tribute to a book.

Huckleberry Finn, with *all* the other books I read as a child, carried me to "bright shore and lonely bay," to more brave new worlds vivid in my imagination. There I spent many a happy hour, while lounging securely in the fastness of bed, school desk, or fireside corner. Reading about Huck, Crusoe, Maggie Tulliver, and other wonderful characters was a joy in those golden days—and reading has continued so, with ever more books, throughout my life. Philosopher Thomas Carlyle has rightly said: "All that mankind has done, thought, gained or been: it is lying as in magic preservation in the pages of books."

My First Day of School

Momentous world events were happening when I started school. Rumblings in Europe boded war, falling markets gave North America its Great Depression, and, more locally, a decade-long drought gripped the Canadian prairies. Saskatchewan was the hardest hit economically, and in mid-province was our sandy farm. We struggled to survive among grasshoppers, dust storms, and parching heat. The year was 1939.

I had turned six that summer and was expected to begin my formal schooling in September, by walking the two miles of trail road to the one-room country school where my brother Ted was in grade eight. He would accompany me along the way each day and help to make me feel more at home in the strange new environment. The problem was that I had no proper clothes to wear.

Playing in the dirt at home, any old scraps of clothing would do: made-over hand-me-downs with patches on patches, and some of them beyond patching. But to start school, to begin an education, to come in contact with a whole new world—this, Mother decided, was not the time to wear cast-off clothing. As the youngest and the last to "leave home" for the halls of learning, I should have a better send-off than that.

There was no money, however, for buying the needed clothing. There was some crop in the field, waiting to be threshed, but until it was safe in the bin or sold at the elevator, it could not entirely be relied upon. Still, conditions were better than two years earlier, when the crop was so sparse it was cut with a mower for feed. Mother determined she would ask the storekeeper in Rosthern for credit till later in fall.

The circumstances involving her decision need to be explained. Farm people did not willingly suspend their feelings of independence and self-reliance. They had a pride in making do and getting by. They did not want or expect aid, only a fair break in market prices and in weather, and they would persevere.

But they had long come to expect that town businesses were not likely to look kindly on unpaid bills, not with so little likelihood of debts ever being paid because of continuing drought. Farmers everywhere were leaving their land on short notice for what they hoped were better stakes up north in the Meadow Lake or Carrot River country. Storekeepers were not promoting "buy-now-pay-later" sales.

So it was with some trepidation that Mother pondered her next move. Of course, she and Dad would have to go into Rosthern, and she would see the storekeeper. (Dad was hard of hearing, and these things were best left to her.) They hitched up one-eyed Beauty and old Tom to the big-wheeled lumber wagon and set off.

There was no box on the wagon that day and my parents sat on the crossbar between the two sets of wheels, jolting along within the dust churned up. It was a time for Mother to think of the appropriate words to say, the approach to take, in pleading her case. She would have it all worked out by the time they got to town.

Within the confines of the store an hour later, with other customers eyeing her, Mother lost her nerve. Her little speech did not sound the same when she went over it in her mind now as it had in the open air of the countryside. She made one motion to catch the storekeeper's attention, clearing her throat as she did so, and then held back.

She tried again, walking forward briskly, hoping that her momentum would carry her along, but at the last instant she swung across to a different aisle and continued walking—out of the store.

"I couldn't do it," she half-laughed but was serious in a moment as she addressed Dad. "We'll have to go home again." She was thinking that she could phone the storekeeper from there. That would be less dificult.

Mother was not one to back down easily, and riding home to the farm strengthened her resolve. While Dad unhitched the horses, she went inside and rang the store's number. There could be no sidestepping this time, and when the storekeeper answered, the words simply tumbled from her.

"Yes, certainly," he broke in, "select whatever you want. That's no problem at all."

"Thank you," Mother said and hung up. She was too exultant to say anything more. The next day she and Dad made another trip to town. The slow, jolting ride was thoroughly enjoyable now, particularly the journey home with brown-paper parcels of new clothing stowed in a box beside them.

In this manner was I smartly accoutered for my first day of school. The main item was a pair of blue-denim bib overalls. Then there was a wine-colored knit shirt, also a navy baseball cap and plain brown running shoes. To complete the outfit, I had a red five-pound Burns lard pail that Mother had saved to be my lunch bucket. (My brother carried a larger syrup pail; he had some new clothes as well.)

What a pair of fine-looking scholars we were on opening day as we strode off, joined by our cousin Jim from a neighboring farm, now walking three abreast down the trail. It would have been a proud—and sad—moment for my mother, watching her lastborn start off to school. I was on the higher middle ground, sometimes half-running through the parched grass there to keep pace with their longer steps along the wheel-worn ruts.

About an hour later we came to the school grounds, where some thirty other students were standing about in small groups, jostling each other good-naturedly and confiding to friends their summer activities, all waiting for the new teacher to ring the bell for nine o'clock.

As luck would have it, I needed to go to the (outside) toilet, and when I came out, there was not one student in sight—just, to a suddenly apprehensive six-year-old, a great empty reach of "well-tramped earth" ("The Prairie School," Isabel Ecclestone Mackay), silent as the outpost-school it surrounded. I rushed across the deserted yard and hesitantly entered the hall of learning. All the students were busy at their desks, and my heart fell within me.

Here on my very first day of school, new clothes notwithstanding, I had committed the most heinous crime of all—being late! I was shattered and stood there, not knowing what to do, seeing my brother look back at me and realizing I had caused him no end of embarrassment.

Fortunately, the teacher rescued me, leading me to an unclaimed single desk at the front of the room, where two other beginners were sitting (grades two and up sat in double desks). They each had a pile of colored wooden pegs on their desks— an inch long, four-sided, and pointed at one end—and now I was given some to occupy my time. I had not seen such things before, and the teacher showed me how to arrange them to create a picture of a house or anything else.

In this way I spent most of my first day at school. The teacher was busy with other classes, introducing them to new work, and we beginners could well quietly amuse ourselves and listen in on the lessons of the other grades. We were gaining awareness of another brave new world.

Of the beginners, I particularly was aware of what was going on around me. Although English was not my first language, I was fluent in it because I had learned it from my older brothers and sister (and parents). The other grade-one students had only the barest knowledge of it. So we played with our pegs—to all of us they were a novel experience.

Before the day was out, the teacher wished, I suppose, to give his beginners a further sense of accomplishment and called us to his desk. There we stood in line facing him. In his hand he held a long yellow pencil, so different from the stubby ones we had at home. I was definitely impressed by its length.

He held it up vertically and, looking about at his young charges, asked us what it was. My mind was made up that I was not going to commit myself, and I looked wonderingly back at him. He furrowed his brow slightly and peered at each of our faces in turn, the intensity of his gaze almost drawing the answer from us—if only it were there. Still, nothing.

"What am I holding here?" he asked again, in a very kind manner. But there was no answer.

Then a light dawned in one of the other beginners. "Pen," he said.

There was a collective sigh of relief from all the students—for naturally they had been watching—and teacher alike. The answer was not quite right, but it was close. We could go back to our seats, the honor of our grade for that day intact.

When school was over and we were walking on the trail once more, I swinging my empty red lard pail, my brother asked me why I had not answered the teacher's question about the pencil. I did not know so I could not tell him, and we walked the rest of the way in silence.

At home there was further interrogation, from my parents and older brother and sister, once I had taken off my new going-to-school clothes and put on everyday garb. Had I liked school?

Had I sat quietly? Had I learned anything?

Yes, I had, and I knew I would continue to go to school and that I would not mind. There would be no end to learning now, despite grasshoppers, drought, and the impending Second World War, which was declared a few days later. My formal education had begun—propitiously, I can now say—thanks to my mother's (and Dad's) foresight and determination. God bless them.

Lunch Bucket Parade

Both our boys' and girls' cloakrooms had a shelf above the coat hooks, extending along one wall and part of the next. On it were arranged, in colorful and crowded display, the pupils' lunch pails. Some of them pyramided neatly atop one another; others perched slantwise and were ready to topple down at the crash of the door. Inside them was our noon-hour meal.

The most common lunch pail was a ten-pound Rogers syrup pail—lunch pails were really *pails* in those days. And the same pail might be handed down from older brother and sister no longer at school to younger siblings when they started.

The Rogers pail was predominantly white with a green and red line painted around the top and bottom edge. The last two colors were repeated in bold lettering for the name of brand and product near the top, with the brand name appearing again, in red script, below. Elsewhere on the cylindrical pail was a drawing of a sugar refinery; also a testimonial, this time in blue letters. Finally, on each pail on the cloakroom shelf were the initials of the pupil, scratched into the white paint.

One reason for its popularity was the ease with which the Rogers pail opened. An inner flange encircled the top edge, and the lid, also flanged, pressed down inside. An older boy with work-toughened hands might simply use his fingernails, claw-like, to pull up the lid. It was better, however, to use the end of a foot-ruler or the blade of a jackknife as a pry to pop the lid open. But another method was wholly reliable. A pupil unhooked the wire handle from its "ears," then placed the middle of the bow under the lid and pried it up. Thus each pail had its own opener.

These pails had another feature to recommend them: they came in different sizes. While the ten-pound variety was just right for carrying the lunch of older individual students, the twenty-pound pail served well if two or three students from one family brought their lunches together. The small five-pound container might carry all the lunch a primary pupil would eat, and he could take pride in having his very own meal. This size, however, lacked a handle.

Burns lard pails also came in varied sizes, suitable for beginning student to big brother or sister. A solid red with an attractive green and gold cloverleaf emblazoned on the sloped side, these pails added more color to the cloakroom-shelf display. And their lids came off easily, too, fitting as they did over the top of the pail. But the pails themselves were less plentiful, if for no other reason than that most farm families in the district butchered their own pigs and so secured their own supply of lard. It was not a generally bought commodity.

Then there were always a few honey pails, navy with white trim. They featured a picture of a conical beehive and the words "Pure Honey" and "Pur Miel" (a honey pail was bilingual; syrup was not). The trouble was that their lids were hard to remove. Deeper than those over syrup, they pressed down directly into the pail, leaving no wide rim to assist leverage.

Finally, there was one lunch bucket the likes of which I have never seen since. It was about a foot long and about half that in width and height. Of gray graniteware, it had rounded corners and a thick wire handle with a wooden grip. Its lid, two inches thick, was a container in itself, sitting on top like a cover on a pot, often filled with a dinnertime drink—milk or cold water. Perhaps this curious "bucket" was intended to be a cooking utensil to be used on a kitchen stove, but if so, it still conveyed lunches admirably.

With better times, regular lunch pails replaced some of those for syrup, lard, and honey, although never wholly so. Brightly painted boxlike containers with hinged lids and two folding handles riveted to the sides appeared. For a time I had a second-hand pail of this sort, but the handles were missing, so I knotted an old shoelace through the holes where the rivets had been.

Other bought lunch pails were those shaped, to us country children, like hip-roofed barns. Black in color, they could hold a thermos bottle in the rooflike lid. However, parents generally thought the purchase of the pail was extravagance enough. The lid could then serve in lieu of a schoolbag, carrying a small book or two or scribblers bent into a half circle. One time, I remember, a schoolmate packed a book I had been carrying, along with his, in this manner on our way to school. The lid on a jar of milk, also in the pail, became loose en route so that the ink from his red-covered *Prester John* stained the cover of my white *Mill on the*

Floss. I was mortified because, while his book came from the school library, the teacher had loaned mine to me.

The lunches that went inside the pails each day could be as varied as the pails themselves. Sandwiches, of course, were a staple, but the bread was always home-baked, and if it was brown, then the flour was home-ground as well. Whole-wheat flour made a solid, gummy, low-risen loaf for which peanut butter made the best spread. Other fillings were whatever leftover meat there was from the previous supper or, in season, vegetables from the garden. A radish sandwich was one of my favorites. Jam sandwiches there were aplenty, too, with the jam—home-canned, naturally—well soaked through the bread by lunchtime. We ate them all with gusto.

A boiled egg provided extra nourishment, and there would be a screw of newspaper, with a mixture of salt and pepper, inside the lunch pail. (Eggs, fried or scrambled, could double as a sandwich filling.) Other lunch-pail "stuffers" were the usual apple or, in later times, an orange, and a cookie or two.

On one occasion I opened my lunch pail to find—a cricket. How it got there, I do not know. Was some schoolmate playing a joke on me? Or did it somehow slip in when the lunch was packed at home? It did not matter. Always the budding naturalist, I felt particularly honored. I felt like Henry David Thoreau when a sparrow alighted upon his shoulder—he was "more distinguished" by that occurrence than "by any epaulet" he could have worn. My cricket, meanwhile, had put me in a holiday picnic mood.

In winter, however, the lunches were eaten at our desks—not exactly a picnic atmosphere, but still a meal away from home. And there could be an outdoor quality to the event if a pupil had forgotten to bring his pail in from the cutter at the school barn and had to eat his sandwiches frozen.

It was the summery weather at the start and close of each school year that made country-school lunches a real treat. Then we sat in a cluster under some shade trees, dipping into our syrup-pail lunch buckets for yet another jam sandwich, leaning back against the solid trunks and contemplating the rural world around us: the extending fields of grain, the winding roads, and the intersecting poplar bluffs. Robins caroled in short bursts from the leafy branches overhead, and butterflies, on frail wings, drifted over the waving grass.

With the letting out of school, the same lunch pails, now empty, were gathered from the cloakroom shelf with a great din as we jostled through the doorway. We were free of classroom studies for another day, striding homeward toward day's end, our strong young bodies well sustained by the simple lunches each pail had held.

Lines by Isabel Ecclestone Mackay in her poem "The Prairie School" complete the picture:

And out of the glow, the children: a whoop and a calling gay,
A clink of lunch-pails swinging as they clash in mimic fray,
A shout and a shouting echo from a world as young as they!

Christmas Holidays

For me, the Christmas holiday season did not begin till our family was riding home from the annual concert at my rural school. Old Tom and one-eyed Beauty pulled our bobsleigh along at a brisk pace through the moonlit winter scene. Jets of steam, flung out by their nostrils, hung about the horses' heads in the cold air as the team, with traces jingling, trotted down the runner-planed road. The sleigh slid along almost effortlessly: it seemed the horses were running and kicking up clods of snow with their hoofs just to stay ahead of it. Occasionally it lurched slightly sideways, then tracked true again to an accompanying squeak of the packed snow underneath.

Dad stood at the front of the sleigh-box—in heavy fur cap, camel-pile coat, and felt packfiller shoes—grasping the reins looped over his huge-mittened hands. Mother sat on a bench along one side—a robe held tightly over her overcoat, a home-knit tam on her head for warmth—tapping her feet under this swaddling of clothes to keep them warm. We children might be snuggled beneath robes on the bench, too, or standing (sometimes hopping about) in the box, looking to all sides.

The snow glistened about us, as the song says, in a winter wonderland of sparkles—snow crystals reflecting the moon's bright light. Yet the bushes we passed looked dark and mysterious, deep woods with ruffed grouse and rabbits snuggled safely under a snow-laden thatch of deadfall and branches. The sky overhead also looked dark and deep, a chill background for its spangle of stars.

The Christmas season at school really started a month before our ride home from the concert. During the last week of November, our teacher canceled the usual Friday afternoon studies and read us sample plays or dramas ("dialogues" we called them), recitations, and acrostics. We children listened with special interest, already deciding which student could best do certain parts. Upon coming to a group agreement, with a lot of teacher guidance, the "parts" were assigned, written out on foolscap by the older students, and handed out early in December. Then the memorization started.

It was fun for some of us to get away to practice a play by ourselves in a cloakroom while the others still had their school work. So we prepared to "trod the stage," but I would not call it a holiday. A holiday was not having to go to school, and now more than anything we had to. Someone's absence meant that the dialogue in which he was cast could not be practiced, and our concert date was fast approaching.

The teacher wisely did not start rehearsals too soon. Not only would we miss more schoolwork that way, but also we could easily be over-rehearsed. Our performance would become stale, lacking the vitality and spontaneity needed to make up for the usual shortcomings of an amateur presentation. Our final rehearsal should still have a few correctable flaws; the concert itself should be the high point of all our efforts.

We started to work at a fever pitch. Plays were performed over and over (by then, several students knew everybody's part); drills were marched out till fatigue set in (and the single record on the portable wind-up gramophone grew scratchy); recitations were recited, songs were sung, and readings were read—all till our voices cracked. It was a relief to do some of the other necessary work.

First we built a stage at the front of the classroom. We brought long planks and supporting two-by-fours up from their basement storage. Each side of the stage needed steps. An over-head wire was strung across the classroom for suspending stage curtains, and shorter wires were strung at right angles for side curtains and dressing rooms.

Then the rest of the classroom was decorated. About fifty streamers fanned out in twisted loops from the center of the ceiling to the picture molding along the walls. These were cut from red, green, and white crêpe paper, with both edges of each streamer crimped by hand to give a serrated look. Some arithmetic tells me that this procedure amounted to about five hundred feet of streamers or a thousand feet of edging, all crimped by students' little fingers.

We cut Christmas designs—stars, candles, angels—out of colored poster paper and pinned them up in a border around the school. Paper bells, opening up like accordions, were hung here and there. Christmas scenes—the Nativity, shepherds with their flocks, Wise Men on camels—were traced on the blackboards and filled in with colored chalk, a fairly complex and time-consuming activity. First the outline drawing was made on brown paper, then the outline pricked out in a series of tiny holes with a pin, then the paper held against the blackboard while someone tapped the lined holes with a dusty chalk brush to transfer the drawing to the blackboard.

So we were busy—acting, reciting, singing (we learned part-singing in groups around the school pedal organ); hammering, sawing, decorating (we climbed up and down trestles like monkeys). Finally concert day arrived, and after one last rehearsal we were dismissed early, to return with our parents and other relatives that evening. The concert was the social event of the year, and everybody came, including people from outside our school district.

There was a special atmosphere to our country school that night. It hardly seemed like a classroom now. We always had some cutters drawn up before the school barn on a regular school day—some students drove in daily—the horses inside the barn. But now, on about the longest night of the year, it was filled not only with cutters but bobsleighs, many with horses still hitched to them, tied to rails, and with blankets thrown over their backs.

Lights shone brightly from the school's row of small-paned windows. Once inside—the men stamping off snow from their boots in the boys' cloakroom, the women combing their hair in the girls'—people could see that all the warm light came from but two mantle lamps, suspended from the ceiling (one above the stage) and hissing away. Planks on little trestles formed most of the seating, while the school desks, shoved to either side, accommodated young mothers and their babies.

A spruce tree with age-old decorations (old even in my time) stood in a front corner. Its prime decorations were real burning candles, and a school trustee—yardstick in hand as a candle-snuffer—sat on guard. The school quickly filled with adults, and students found their places on the front benches. The children sat in order so that they could march up and at once form a smart-looking school chorus.

Lights, streamers, bells, candles, the tree (yes, the teacher and students must have worked hard); whispers backstage—someone saying sh-sh-sh ("Is everybody here?"); opening curtains, the teacher walking center stage, a moment of hushed waiting ("Ladies and gentlemen, parents, boys, and girls ... ")—let the play begin.

So followed choruses, drama, drills, and poems. To us children/performers, they seemed to go by in rapid-fire order. There was no time for appraisal, suggestions, a second chance. This was it: say your lines and make way for the next part of the program. We each counted the items still to come before our big moment onstage took place. We were just swept along, and then—the concert was over. We had barely had time to notice the finery we all self-consciously wore on this special occasion, some girls having their hair curled for the first time, some boys feeling awkward in bow ties.

Then Santa Claus made his appearance, clanging the school bell and *ho-ho*ing his way upstage. There were gifts to distribute (students had exchanged names) and bags of goodies for all pupils and preschoolers. With a scrounging in bags to see what was there (a chocolate bar was a unique yearly treat), and a rustling of tissue paper from opened gifts (the paper was saved for gift-wrapping next year), and then saying thank you—children began to wrestle an arm into a sleeve of a mackinaw or jacket. The hectic preparations of the last weeks were ending in another rush of activity: finding one's boots and cap and mittens.

Families filed out of the schoolhouse at last, wishing each other "Merry Christmas," and made their way to waiting bobsleigh or cutter and blanketed horses. Our team was as impatient to be gone as any of them. Clutching my bag of peanuts and candy in one hand and keeping a tight hold of my gift under my arm—one year, I remember, it was a storybook about Babe Ruth—I crawled into the sleigh-box with the others of my family. Dad said "giddap" to the horses, and we drove off into the night.

No more hustle or bustle, no more lines of play or recitation to remember, no more wearing of "Sunday" clothes—at least for a while. Just a week to ten days of doing nothing—except the usual farm chores—eating good food, playing great games, reading new books, skiing cross-country, building snow forts, skating outdoors, listening to the radio, visiting friends. All these things I anticipated as the horses clopped along, as the bobsleigh runners swished through the snow. The moon shone down brightly; the landscape glowed as if with an inner light. Warm thoughts filled me completely as we raced toward home in the cold night air. My real holidays were just beginning. I tried to savor each moment.

Play Ball!

1

Despite the umpire's call of "Play ball!" softball was hardly a matter of *play* to a farm boy in the olden days. It was serious business.

Our school—grades one to eight with a few nine and ten correspondence students—had two ball diamonds: one, regulation-size with a backstop; the other, somewhat smaller and off in a far corner. Primary-grade students played on the junior diamond, learning the skills of the game merely by playing every day at recess. Scores were kept only casually, however earnestly we played.

The senior diamond held hotly contested games, with players assiduously filling out and monitoring a scorecard as each team came up to bat. The sides were usually chosen each morning, and play continued over two recesses and the noon hour. Intervening classroom studies were needed rest periods, a time of renewal before scrambling down the school steps to re-enter the playground fray.

Sometimes when the base paths were wet from an infrequent rain and not fit for running, everyone played knock-out-flies together in the outfield of the big diamond. There the smaller students showed their eagerness by chasing those wayward fly balls that rolled far beyond the knot of fielders. Of course, when a catchable fly was hit, no amount of enthusiasm ensured a junior's catching it, for an older student was there, too, with a much longer reach.

Then one day it happened. An older student tapped a promising youngster on the shoulder and said, "You better come and play on the big diamond." Just like that. No initiation endured or certificate given. But that tap on the shoulder was a coming of age and a rite of passage. One had graduated to the "big diamond" and, with quiet self-control, basked in the glory for weeks.

Play in the "big league" was no easy matter. The other players were not only older but also bigger and stronger and more skilled. Practice and yet more practice—on the school ground, at home with a brother or sister, by oneself with a sponge ball— would hone the skills, but only time and wholesome farm foods could make up for the lack in size and strength. A bigger student could simply hit the ball farther, run faster, and catch better with his longer legs and larger hands. In so doing he would also intimidate and rattle a youngster.

So the rite of passage meant being an underling for a year or two, sometimes humiliated by one's inept play, but always persevering and improving. A pupil knew that the ball diamond was a testing ground of his mettle, and with continued practice and dedication he would make the school team, the "select nine." Then he could play against other school teams, in exhibition or superintendency-playoff games, and even against "outsiders," those young men of the same school district who had already left school.

There were many such "graduates" then, needed at home to do farm work when much of it was manual labor, who missed the camaraderie of school sports and were only too anxious to take on us "insiders" at the annual last-day-of-school picnic. Most of them had been our school companions just a few years before, but some older ones were present also, still willing to demon strate their softball skills. For an evening exhibition game with another school, they turned up *en masse* to cheer on their home school and to applaud a younger brother on the playing field.

When I was in grade six and had been playing on the team for a couple of years, our school had the makings of a very good "select nine." The next year, when we were all a year older and stronger still, we would win the superintendency championship in a thrilling 2-1 ballgame and also beat the outsiders on picnic day. But it was the previous year, when I was still in grade six, that featured the most memorable game of all.

2

It came about in this way. One of our grade-eight students lived outside the rural school district, on a farm but in the area falling under the local town school, a twelve-room edifice in Rosthern. He and his siblings attended our school, as it was closer, but he still had some contact with goings-on in town. He had told a few Rosthern students about our ball team, and they, knowing that he was in grade eight and that we had a grade-nine player as well, said they would get up a team to match and come down to play us some evening. A time and date were fixed.

The rest of our team found this news a little disconcerting. In those days the urban-rural split occurred at the farm gate. People who lived in town were clustered together, with sidewalks and electricity and nearby stores. The students, when not in school, hung about the cafés or strolled the streets.

The older players on our team (all of thirteen or fourteen years) said that they were not going to be fazed by any town kids, but some of us younger ones were not so sure. We all had heard them use the epithet, "You farmer," when they wanted to taunt anyone rural, and my first acquaintance with their world five years earlier had not been the most pleasant.

For some reason I had been standing alone off Main Street when a welcoming committee of town youngsters, somewhat older than I, had suddenly surrounded me, wanting to know where my father was. It was my ingenuousness that saved me. I could not know that with my father (and protector) absent, they had hoped to lure or chase me into an alley, where one of them would pick a fight while the others jeered and pranced around in high glee at the spectacle. So I had answered coolly and unconcernedly that he was at the grain elevator. I had just stood there, relaxed, waiting for some other questions, while they, nonplussed, had wandered off. Would we be playing against some of these same boys, now adolescents?

To us in our rural innocence, they were a bunch of "toughies," even as to them in their urban sophistication, we were a bunch of "rubes"—although we did not know the word then. The game would be more than just a match between two schools.

The anticipated evening finally came. Our team members had hurried home from school on foot, bicycle, or buggy; finished their chores—milking cows, chopping wood, feeding pigs; gulped a quick supper; then walked or ridden back to the school grounds. There was still plenty of time. Coming along were older brothers (the outsiders), sisters, and mothers and fathers, too. It seemed that most of the district was there.

Our team did a little warming up on the senior diamond before the opposing team made its appearance. Our players included every boy at school from grades five to nine. Our catcher and biggest player—the only student from grade nine—was Peter, a stocky individual and a solid rock on defence. Then there were two students from grade eight, playing first base and center field. Of three grade-seven students, one played left field and the other two alternated between pitcher and shortstop. I, from grade six, was on second base. Two grade-five pupils filled out the team at third base and right field.

All of us batted right-handed so that right field was considered the easiest position to play. Few balls were hit in that direction, and a newcomer to the team usually started there. Our smallest player, Elmer, patrolled that field, and his play, like Peter's, would be important to the outcome of the game.

Since everybody batted right-handed, we were not particularly concerned with the schoolyard fence that ran behind first base, parallel with a line from home plate to center field. Seldom would a fair ball clear the fence, and when one did it was automatically called a ground-rule double. That feature also would have an important bearing on the game.

And then the town team arrived—in a truck that one of the boys' fathers used for delivering groceries. It rolled onto the yard, horn honking, and students waving wildly from the box at the back or shouting from the two running boards, where some of them stood: "We're here! We're here! We're here!"

They certainly were, along with several hangers-on. When they all piled off the truck and stood around us, we wondered which of them would be our opponents. We could not see any small students anywhere. When the team members bunched together around their equipment, we finally understood what was in store for us. This team was chosen solely from grades eight and nine, about half and half—big fellows all of them, the best from their school.

There was nothing we could do now. The game was scheduled, the crowd waiting. An umpire was selected, scorecards were drawn up, and an upright bat was flung from one captain to the other—to be gripped upward along its handle by the two players in turn, one hand at a time. The last one to clasp the bat could choose "bats" or "fields" to start the game.

Peter, our captain, won the bat toss and decided to have our team field first. This had always been the wiser choice, as we would be last to bat at the end of the game. But on this day it would prove otherwise.

3

"Play ball!" the umpire called, and we took our positions. The crowd, sympathetic to us, was silent, waiting to see what would happen.

We all felt a little shaky in the field, facing these confident town players who swung their bats menacingly during warm-up. The worst part, we would soon find out, was that a good number of them batted left-handed. I usually had a pretty good sense of where a ball might be hit from watching the batter's approach to the plate or his stance there, but now I was baffled, as were the other fielders. The hitter's big right shoulder and forearm seemed to be hiding the bat from us, and we could not figure out how the ball would be struck.

Then came the sharp hits, through holes in our defence; runners filled the bases and runs were scored before we got even one batter out—the town players were prancing about with glee. Five runs crossed home plate, and the bases were still loaded when the side was retired. It was the short right-field fence and its compensating ground rule that helped us. Their left-handed batters had twice hit fair balls over the fence.

"That's just one inning," Peter consoled us when we came off the field. "Now it's our turn."

But we were still shaky, if not shell-shocked, and went out one-two-three. "We'll get 'em next time," Peter said.

Back in the field, the town's hitting barrage continued, along with a great deal of huzzahs and laughter from their hangers-on as the game seemed to be turning into a rout. Our huge supporting crowd had nothing to cheer about yet. Three more runs crossed the plate, and the score was 8 to 0 when we came up to bat the second time.

Our first batter now was the grade-eight student who had

arranged the game and thus may have felt called upon to get a hit. He slashed a hard grounder at the shortstop. The fielder bobbled the ball, and we had our initial runner on base. The crowd had held back long enough, and an excited buzzing was everywhere behind us, if only because of an opposition error.

The pitcher must have thrown the same pitch to our next batter, Peter, the catcher. He lifted a high fly ball between two outfielders and drove in a run.

Now the crowd was wildly cheering—but not for long. The pitcher bore down again, and the next three batters went out.

Still, it felt better trotting out into the field. At least we were on the scoreboard; we would not be skunked.

Things were working out better for us defensively, too. Usually the palms of my hands sweated from nervous excitement and made the inside of my small glove moist. For me that was good: the glove then seemed to be a part of my hand and worked with it. My hands were sweaty now—let any line drive or grounder come my way!

We were getting our confidence back, and left-handed batters no longer seemed to be quite such a mystery. One hit an extremely high pop fly, and the pitcher motioned to me to take it. I circled underneath as it began to drift out sideways, beyond my territory, but I stayed with it and made the catch. I was now relaxed and felt that I was really in the game.

Although the town team got some runners on base that inning, none scored, and we came in to the bench feeling not too bad. If only we had not let in all those early runs!

So play continued for a couple of innings, neither team scoring, but a few plays bringing the crowd alive. One was a line smash off the bat of the biggest player on the town team. He had swung his bat intimidatingly in the on-deck circle and swaggered to the plate with a blunt "OK, you farmers, this is how you play ball." He liked to act the real "toughie" and had power to back up his bluster.

His hit cracked against the school wall, but our left fielder was Johnny-on-the-spot, playing the carom perfectly, smartly fielding the ball, and getting it to me at second. The batter, meanwhile, was lumbering around first, not realizing he had been cut off, and continued running. Now I was his welcoming committee, though I tapped him only lightly for the out.

When we got in to bat, an outsider was waiting for us. "I've been watching your swings," he said. "When you got that run before, I noticed Peter step into the pitch. Maybe that's what all of you should be doing. I think the pitcher is getting you a little off stride and you want that extra jump."

Well, we tried it and it seemed to help. Some of us went out, but we got a few runners on base, and the crowd was getting more excited.

The next time around, the score still 8 to 1, we had the bases loaded, with two out, when Peter came up to bat. He had got our only extra-base hit so far, and the outfielders started backing up. The pitcher checked their positions before stepping back onto the mound.

The crowd was in a hopeful frenzy, razzing the retreating fielders, shouting instructions to the batter, but it was just a melee of sound breaking over us on the bench as our concentration shifted from our captain alone at the plate to the playing field with its opposing team.

4

Then came the pitch—and Peter swung. There was a hush, an explosive crack, and then a welling up of noise, a crescendo this time, as the ball took flight. All the years of after-school chores— milking cows, walking after plodding horses behind a harrow, pitching bundles in the fall—all the strength that this work gave to muscle and sinew in thigh and back, neck, shoulder, and forearm was concentrated in that split-second collision of circling bat and curving ball.

The ball sailed high into the blue sky—on and on, over the gaping fielders, as though free at last, never to come down. The runners scampered around the bases, and the ball arced earthward finally, making a rushing sound, to thud into the chaff and straw before the barn at the end of the schoolyard where the buggies stood.

The next batter went out, but the score was now 8 to 5. We were in the ball game again, and there were still three innings to go.

Again we held the opposition scoreless, for by now we were all playing above our heads as if in a dream. Our center fielder went back on a fly ball, turned sideways, hoping the ball would be there, and saw it land in his outstretched glove. And he hung on. It was a great catch, preventing a run from scoring.

At bat once more, we continued to "step into the pitch." Again we had runners on board, two of them, and now our first baseman was up. It was he who had scored the first run and he who was our second-best power hitter. That this game was being played was his doing; here was his chance to do something about the result.

Perhaps he had no thought of being a standard bearer for the rural community against the urban world—after all, he was friends with some of the opposition players. Perhaps he was just trying to show that he could belong to that world, too. He swung his bat forcefully at the incoming pitch, struck true, and the ball sailed into left field and rolled along the edge of the poplar bluff there. Three more runs came home, and the score was tied.

So it stood into the next, the second last, inning. The crowd was alive to every pitch. The ball was hit, caught, thrown to first. Batters came up, went out; but some were safe, too. Again we were playing as in a dream, where the actual plays seemed fated, beyond our control.

With runners in scoring position, our "rookie," little Elmer, in the outfield, made the fielding gem of the day. A fly ball in short right field seemed out of reach, a lucky hit, but Elmer came running in and, going all out, made a barehanded catch at his ankles. (As the youngest player on our team, he did not even have a glove.) The runners had to hold.

He had had no right to make that catch, not a ten-year-old boy with small hands reaching down to his shoelaces for the dropping ball. But we had all been playing as though inspired from the third inning on, and we just touched our caps to acknowledge the play and got the rest of the batters out.

Elmer was beside himself with excitement when we came in to bat. He was simply thrilled with his catch—whatever element luck had played in it—and happy we could hold our own with those "town guys."

And now it was his turn to bat. It seemed, crouching at the plate, that he was grinning too much to concentrate on hitting the ball. His luck (and new-found skill), however, was not deserting him just yet.

The pitcher whipped two fast pitches by him—both called balls by the umpire—then looped a rainbow throw toward the plate, saying, "Here, little farmer, see if you can hit that."

Had Elmer swung away, he would have missed, but he hesitated for an instant, *stepped into the pitch* like his role models, and swung mightily. He caught just a piece of the ball, squibbing it off his bat, and it spun crazily down the base path, while he was off immediately, scooting ahead of it, like a frisky calf, down to first base—safely.

The crowd was shouting and waving, just going frantic, and Elmer was hopping about first base, now wildly thrilled with his very latest accomplishment.

"C'mon, Elmer!" someone in the crowd cried out, and others chimed in. The noise was stupendous.

The next batter positioned himself in the batter's box, and down came the first pitch, *whack* into the catcher's mitt—and off went Elmer toward second base. It was bad softball, trying to steal second like that, and the crowd was hysterical. In the bedlam, the catcher, caught totally off guard, fumbled the ball and could not get his throw away in time.

Elmer slid safely into second, uncontested as it were, and bounced up onto his new base, cocky as a bantam rooster. The crowd was beside itself, and one of our players not up for bat, who had been coaching at first, threw up his hands in disbelief.

"Hey, what's that little kid doing on second base?" the catcher said to cover up his error and drew a laugh from the partisan crowd. Some of the town-rural animosity seemed to be breaking down for the moment, and we enjoyed the humor.

Another outsider now worked his way into our ranks at the bench. He could hardly contain himself. "'That little kid' might just win the game for us," he said and told us he would take over coaching at third—there was too much on the line to have one of us do it now—and he hurried to the diamond without a pause or comment from us.

"Hold it, Elmer," the new coach called across the diamond. "Wait! Wait till you've got a good chance to run." He gestured with both hands up in the air. Elmer continued hopping about the base, first on one foot, then on the other. He was ready to go.

The next pitch was hardly on its way before Elmer was off again, despite all the coach's remonstrations. The batter swung and hit an infield ground ball. Would Elmer be caught in a rundown? No, there was only one play for the infield, and that was to first base. Elmer was now safely on third.

"Wait till I tell you to leave," the third-base coach said again. He was not thinking of Elmer's second base-running mistake or of his own frantic efforts to have the runner hold. Elmer was on third, and that was all that mattered. "We can get you home on a fly ball, even if it's caught, but you can't leave the base before that. Remember, you can't leave the base before that."

Elmer smiled up affectionately. He liked his coach's attention but knew that he was going to score a run, whatever instruction he received—just as everybody else was beginning to know. The momentum was building, and nothing could stop it.

The next few pitches were deliberate balls—the pitcher was trying to regain control of the game—but then came a fast ball over the corner of the plate, and our batter swung and sent a lazy fly ball into deep center field. It would be caught, but Elmer tagged up and scampered on home with the go-ahead run.

He was one big smile, and the rest of us were smiling too, patting him on the head and hoping our luck would hold for one more inning—because the final batter on our side had just grounded out. Boy, what a ball game!

"Take it easy," our new coach said as we headed back to the field.

5

There had been many ball games played before our epic struggle with the urban Goliaths, and there have been many more played since, but our contest never lacked in drama till the final out. The first batter for the town team was none other than its star player, who had cracked a line drive off the schoolhouse and been thrown out at second base. He again took his stance at the plate and repeated his "OK, you farmers, this is how you play ball."

He looked at a couple of pitches and then found one to his liking. The resounding crack on contact was tremendous, and the ball was on its way. He had pulled the hit to right field, where it flew over helpless Elmer's head, still gaining altitude and continuing on its flight path, finally beginning to curve downward gradually, hooking more and more to the right as it went, and then plumping to ground in fair territory but just *over the fence*.

It was the farthest-hit ball I had ever seen at our senior diamond, considerably farther than Peter's home run—it seemed to go a mile while the crowd watched with hushed disbelief—but it was only a long, long ground-rule double. There was a collective expiration of withheld breath from all the spectators, players and crowd, when the ball landed.

The disappointed batter jogged to second and sat down on the plate. He had deserved a better fate than that. Still, he was in scoring position and there were none out. Our job was to keep the run from scoring.

The crowd helped us now, cheering on our valiant pitcher, jeering at the dejected runner. "Old Tubby," as they called the player at second base, was standing once more, waiting for something to happen.

But the next batter popped out. "Hey, Tubby, what's the attraction at second base? Don't you want to leave?"—these were the calls hurled at the runner.

When the next batter struck out, "Tubby" was the butt of more fun: "Are you tired out and can't run anymore? Try *stealing* third." The crowd was sensing victory and having a good time.

We in the field still seemed to be in a fantasy world. Just one more batter to go, yes, but could we get him out? We all stood poised intently at our positions and waited for the hit as each pitch hurled toward the plate.

Then it came, a fast grounder between first and second, and I loped toward it. The play seemed so completely natural. All the times I had thrown a sponge ball against our granary wall and then immediately charged ahead to field the rebound had sharpened my reflexes for just such a play. Now I kept my eye on the bounding ball, hands held loosely before me in readiness, as I unconcernedly (or so it seemed again) intercepted its course. Then I flipped it over to first base for the final out.

The game was over, and we could at last shake off the veil of dreams that had hung over us. This was not a fairy tale but a real live happening—on our own schoolyard and before an appreciative crowd. We had won: Country 9, Town 8.

Brothers, sisters, mothers, and fathers were too worn out from all the excitement to do much cheering anymore. They mingled with us on the playing field, patting us on the shoulder or just giving us a knowing nod. We had done it, done the impossible, beaten a team much stronger and bigger than we were.

The town players stood aside, rather out of place, not knowing what to do next, then started to gather up their equipment and wander off to their truck. "Aw, shucks, we should have won," one of them said.

"Tubby," their star player, turned around at that point and walked back to us. He had a sheepish grin on his face. "Hey, that was all right," he said, sticking out his hand to Peter in congratulations. "Good game, you guys," he added, turning around to the whole team—"all except for him over there," and he pointed his chin at Elmer. "That's not how you play ball."

Elmer smiled broadly at that, and even the rest of us, we jubilant "rubes," nodded in agreement. We did not mind a little kidding.

"We'll get you in another game—don't you worry," Tubby continued, and he started to walk away. "We should have won, you know."

And, of course, they should have. But they had not. On that day, on that evening, on that ball diamond to which all of us rural students had aspired to play and to excel, we "farmers" had won. We had won with the timely hitting of our captain and our liaison first baseman, with the daring base running of our rookie right fielder, and with the superb fielding plays of each one of us.

Sometimes everything in life comes together for one splendid and glorious moment, never to be forgotten. We had had such a moment in time, and we would keep the memory of it with us always—of a golden evening when we had responded seriously to the call of "Play ball!" and had played better than we knew.

Country Roads

Sixty-five years ago our rural roads had "grass between" where wagon wheels had made parallel trails in the prairie sod (I still enjoy wandering along such roads although they are not common now), and wagons and buggies were far more plentiful than cars. The sight of a transport truck driving past our school afforded conversation for several days' recesses. Later, teams took to driving in the grassy ditch along highways to escape the motor traffic. At driveways into farmyards or fields, the teamster would have to swing onto the graveled road before resuming his course along the ditch.

Natives and Métis on their way from Duck Lake or Batoche to Rosthern were frequent ditch drivers. Their trips, however short, always seemed to be adventurous excursions. A few miles from town there was a poplar bluff beside the road. Often I saw a Native family camped there—halted for an afternoon's picnic before continuing the journey. A white canvas tent was pitched against the green bush, the driver within, checking out some gear. His wife was bending over a fire, and the children were watching her. The horses, unhitched but not unharnessed, were champing grass and lazily swishing flies. Life was slower in those days, and there was no hurry to cover the dozen or so miles to home.

In winter the busiest road coming out of Rosthern left town at the old power house, no longer standing, and proceeded east over two small iron bridges spanning a winding creek, before going a short distance south and turning east again, to follow the boundary line between farms. It passed through the middle of a farmer's yard, between house and barn, and went on straight east until it had to skirt a meadow rimmed with bushes. Till then, the trail had followed the same road as used in summer, but here it began to cut across fields, first my uncle's, then ours. It continued cross-country eastward to the South Saskatchewan River and beyond, leaving seams side by side in the snow, packed hard by horses' hoofs and worn shiny by iron-bound sleigh runners.

During some winters in the 1920s, caravans of bobsleighs hauling ice passed by our yard. The blocks of ice were sawn at the river and taken to town, where they were used in iceboxes, the forerunners of refrigerators. Even after these modern appliances became more common, ice was still used by some of the local merchants—the butcher, for instance. Ice was also cut from a frozen pond on the old Derksen farm southeast of town. When this nearby source was exhausted, the teams had to make the longer haul from the river and so drove up and down our winter road again.

In my boyhood the road was much used to haul loads of wood to town as well. Selling firewood was a chief source of winter income for many of the farmers who lived across the river. Into the poplar bluffs on their windswept fields or the wooded draws leading down to the river, the men waded through the loosely drifted snow, axes in hand, to disturb the wintry stillness with their chopping. Their teams of horses, each hitched to only a set of bobsleigh runners, waited outside the bush. Jets of condensing vapor streamed from the horses' nostrils.

The sleighs, piled with logs to a height of three or four feet, crossed our farm, their bundled-up drivers sitting on top, guiding the plodding teams. (Before my time, the teams often were oxen.) In town they parked on a vacant lot north of the railway station to wait for customers. The drivers stood by, trying to look confident when townspeople walked up to examine the logs. A load generally sold for three dollars.

Poor frail humanity! Some sleigh loads concealed a twisted tree trunk in the center so that a buyer had to look at the logs from the ends to make sure he was getting a full load, not a hollow one. On the other hand, some townspeople would not buy their wood until late in the afternoon. By then the poor drivers, cold from standing beside their loads for several hours and needing money to buy groceries, would be forced to sell their wood for perhaps two dollars or even at half price. There was no point in taking it home.

There was a lot of other traffic on the winter road. On either of the two busiest market days, Thursday and Saturday, thirty to forty sleighs would cross our farm. Our trail was a main stream, not a tributary, many side roads having fed into it.

The reason for this "thoroughfare" was that old ways were slow to change. The road had begun as an ox-cart trail linking Rosthern to Fish Creek across the river, channeling traffic from the large Ukrainian settlement there and from even more distant points such as Alvena. This continued when I was a boy, except where fences and pastures altered its course. The original trail had gone by the corner of our barn, and traces of it can still be seen in the virgin sod of our pasture.

Having a well-traveled trail past our door had its advantages, apart from hitching rides on occasion. There were of course the times when my mother hailed a passing buggy in summer and the travelers not only took our can of cream into town but also returned in the late afternoon with the check from the creamery. Another time Mother wished to return a mail-order hat. Again she hailed a passing team. The Ukrainian woman on it could understand no English, but Mother pointed to the box and said, "Eaton's." She also pointed to the corner on which postage should be placed and gave the woman the required money. The woman smiled broadly and nodded her head. Likely, she, too, knew the difficulties of ordering clothes through the mail.

And now—where are these neighbors? Where are the bending country roads they traveled, the ones with "grass between"? For the most part they have come to an end in our fast-paced world—save for that nostalgic "a-winding into the land of [our] dreams …"

A Boy and His Bicycle

Today, children have little chance to *anticipate* owning a bicycle. Even preschoolers scoot along sidewalks on scaled-down models with training wheels. As for bicycles, they seem readily available. In my boyhood, however, we longed for them first, dreamed of them, perhaps for years.

I had learned early that pedaling a bicycle was a speedy means of bringing far horizons near. Walking was slow going with small, boyish steps, but a bicycle had wings: my much older brother, Ernie, had cycled as far as Christopher Lake, eighty miles distant, along poor gravel roads in the late 1930s; the trip had taken him from parched prairie into humid boreal forest in a single day. While I had nothing that grandiose in mind, I did envision excursions to the shaded coolness of the purling South Saskatchewan, six miles away. With a bicycle I could be a fisherman, independent, pursuing this "trade" on my own of a summer's day, responsibly providing fare for the family table while having a keen adventure to boot.

In my grade three *Highroads* reader I had learned of the exultation of "Going Down Hill on a Bicycle." In this wonderful poem, Henry Charles Beeching spoke of the cyclist's sensations, poised on top of a hill and then coasting down. "The air goes by in a wind," he wrote.

The second stanza best described the "exultation":

Swifter and yet more swift,
Till the heart with a mighty lift
Makes the lungs laugh, the throat cry:—
"O bird, see; see, bird, I fly."

For a "golden moment," the rider shared the bird's "feathery life in air." Whoever climbed the highest hill found "wings waiting."

So I longed for a bicycle—for those reasons that boys of still previous generations wanted a horse. Poet James Thomson said in 1869: "Give a man a horse he can ride," and "his rank and wealth, his strength and health" shall not fail. A bicycle to ride would give me, too, a kind of rank, if not wealth (although, maybe, I could run some errands), and surely strength and health as well from pedaling the many miles I intended to travel.

Oliver Wendell Holmes, in 1834, said, in related vein: "It makes men imperious to sit a horse." While I would try not to be domineering or overbearing when sitting on my bicycle, I knew that I could not help feeling, would in fact take pride in knowing, that I was now someone of worth. As on a horse, one could sit tall on a bicycle saddle.

I waited to have a bicycle all my own. In the interval I prepared myself by learning to ride—one has to be able to stay *on* the saddle before one can sit tall. My cousin Jim of about the same age already had a bike, so between the two of us—his steady guidance in running alongside, trying to hold the shaking contrivance upright; my unwitting counteraction on the saddle, attempting to coordinate hands, feet, and a "sitting-tall" posture (before giving way to gravity at last)—we persevered. Despite scraped knees and elbows and bruised shins, neither of us would give up, and a few days of focused effort finally led to my first successful solo circling of the farmyard.

To celebrate, my cousin announced that he would type out an "official" certificate of my achievement on his family's old Oliver typewriter. We alternated riding his bicycle back to his

place—the one not riding trotted in the second wagon track—
and there set about our secretarial business. The document, in
faded type, began: "This is to certify that ..."

We immediately returned to my house, in the same ride-and-
jog fashion, to show the certificate to my mother and dad. Dad,
partly deaf and not always fully aware of all we were up to, had
here visual proof of my accomplishment. He and Mother nodded in smiling agreement—yes, it was time, now that I could
"officially" ride, for me to have a bicycle of my own.

The bicycle, of course, would be second-hand—that fact
went unsaid. Although we were several years into the Second
World War, our quarter-section farm was still in debt. The trouble was that there were no second-hand bikes to be had. Because
of the war effort, no new bicycles were being manufactured, and
so old bicycles, those still in repair, were retained by whoever was
lucky enough to have one.

Mother was not taken aback. Now that she and Dad had
made their decision, she began telephoning all the neighboring
farm households to see if, by some chance, an old bicycle might
happen to be stashed away, half-forgotten, in somebody's granary or other outbuilding. Her circle of inquiry became wider and
wider, but there was just no bicycle for sale anywhere, it seemed.

Our next step was to pore over the classified advertisements
in the two farm weeklies we received. Perhaps someone somewhere had a used bicycle for sale. Then one week there it was—
"FOR SALE: Bicycle ..." The address given was halfway across the
province.

In those days, people responded to advertisements by letter.
No telephone number was even given, for ordinary folks would
certainly not spend money on a long-distance call just to trans-
act some business. Long-distance calls were for emergencies or
maybe a death in the family—not for frivolous things like buying
a bicycle.

Mother, however, was ahead of her time. Because of the distance, a letter from us would definitely not be the first one to

arrive; with bicycles in demand, there would be prospective buyers much closer at hand. So Mother telephoned long distance. First she had to inquire through several operators (or "centrals," as they were called then) whether the people with the bicycle indeed had a telephone. Yes, they had, and Mother spoke directly to them. I remember the family's name yet.

Naturally, Mother was the first person to "answer" the advertisement. Having been assured that the bicycle was in working order, she agreed to the price named and arranged to have the item shipped by train on a C.O.D. (cash on delivery) basis. Coming away from the wall telephone rather flustered (again, long-distance calls were not an everyday event), she had a gleam in her eye. She had stolen a march on any letter writers wanting that bicycle. Now the waiting began—but it was a *short* wait, and for a definite bicycle.

A week went by, but nothing arrived at the railway station in town for us. A second week—still nothing. What could have happened?

Mother got on the telephone once more. The same man on the other end was hardly apologetic. After her first phone call, he said, someone had come by to look at the bicycle and had offered him cash on the spot; he had accepted it. That way he did not need to bother taking the bicycle to the railway station to ship it.

But a deal had been made and he had promised to send it, Mother said, nonplussed.

"Well, yes …," he agreed, but there was really nothing more to say, and Mother hung up.

She and Dad were as disappointed as I was, and now the *long* wait from before continued.

No more bicycles came up for sale over the whole of the next year. Then one day in the summer of 1945, when the war was ending, Dad and I were in the hardware store in town. Dad mentioned to the owner the difficulty of getting me a used bicycle.

"Well," said the owner, "I'm getting in two *new* bicycles, a boy's and a girl's, if one of those will do."

This came as a real surprise. New bicycles had been absent for so long that their existence had not even been considered—by anybody in the town or surrounding district, apparently. Nobody had spoken for either bicycle, and the store owner had a funny little smile on his face. It seemed he had been waiting for just such an opportune moment to announce their imminent arrival.

The timing was favorable for us, too. In the interval since our failed attempt to buy the used bicycle, my parents had paid for our farm, and there was some money on hand. Dad made a down payment, and we left the store. After all my years of waiting, I was going to get a new bicycle.

A few months later it came. No unkept promise this time. It was there one Saturday night when we made our weekly trip to town. Dismantled, it was in a large flat cardboard box, with straps of steel binding it fast. We tied the box down, resting it on the back bumper of our Model A, and rambled on home. It was too late that evening to do anything with it, however.

The next morning, my parents were up long before I was so that, on my arising, the new bicycle was already in one piece, leaning against the summer kitchen, with sunlight gleaming from its enameled surfaces. My bike was a rich wine color, with cream mud-guards and chrome handlebars. And it was a C.C.M.—the finest bicycle to be had in those days.

My longing, my waiting, was over. My dream of owning a bicycle had become reality. Now I could sail like a bird, the experience making "the lungs laugh, the throat cry" in the rushing wind. I had "wings waiting" to bring far horizons near—to ride to the river for a day's fishing, to ride to town for groceries if need be, to venture on and on, gaining "strength and health" as I did so. And the rank I now attained—free, independent, riding tall in the bicycle saddle, gazing down on the world from an elevation of a foot or so—gave me a new perspective. Splendid and glorious days were before me.

Actually, the trails I cycled along at the time were so sandy that the bottom of each turning wheel was sometimes entirely buried. Little chance then of "flying" downhill, but, never mind, I was undaunted. I enjoyed the gentle coasting ride, even though I had to stand up on the pedals to have enough power to gain the top of the hill in the first place.

As for the feeling of the air going by "in a wind," that happened often enough when I had straight-going on a hard stretch of road and really spun the pedals. Winds on our prairies, I found, always seemed to be blowing, and for half of any ride they were against the cyclist. Then it was bending low over the handlebars, to cut down wind resistance, and pumping down on the pedals again with all my might. Yet I was entirely thrilled with having a bicycle. I did make some trips to the river and to town—huge adventures each one of them—and I rode to our country school every day.

Sometimes a fellow student would drop by on his own bicycle of an evening. Though we had both ridden several miles to and from school earlier in the day, we would ride some more, making a whole loop of municipal roads encircling eight quarter sections—another six miles of up-and-down hills and sandy tracts, with mosquitoes streaming by. But there were the coolness of evening, the moist scents of the roadside grasses, the

gold and tawny western sky, and the great night coming on. Somehow, not seeing the road ahead clearly in the growing darkness seemed to smooth away the ruts and bumps and tire-enveloping sand. We were sharing a bird's, a night bird's, "feathery life in air," coursing along, homeward bound.

Grade twelve, my only year of high school attendance in town, was my last occasion to ride my bicycle extensively. I rode four miles west to school over cross-country trails each morning and returned home each evening. As the fall days grew shorter, I left before sunup and, halfway to town, began to feel the sun's warmth on my back—while my hands, within my own shadow, remained chilled gripping the handlebars. The world was one of pale sunlight and long shadows, with migrating sparrows lisping in the bushes and vs of geese and cranes calling overhead, all journeying along, too. Cycling to school made me at one with nature's inhabitants, sensing their world, enjoying a time of stillness and peace before my studies for the day began.

Now, half a century later, I can relive those wonderful bicycle days in my memory, the boyhood pleasures of owning and riding a bike. And I still have that same bicycle—in more or less new condition. Sometimes I pump up the tires and take it for a spin.

When I back the bicycle out of the garage, I remind myself to mount cautiously—I am not as young as I used to be. Then, in starting away, without thinking, I have stepped on the near pedal and flung my other leg over the saddle and am sailing off, down the paved street, "swifter and more swift," once more that boy I was, once more living that "golden moment":

"O bird, see; see, bird, I fly."

Saturday Night in Town

"There was a special pleasure and excitement ... when Saturday night trading was a part of country living." So wrote Haydn S. Pearson, a New Hampshire countryman, in an essay from *The New England Year* (1966). His words held true as well for prairie folks each summer, particularly in the second half of the 1940s.

What really made Saturday night in town a weekly custom was horse-and-wagon travel giving way to the automobile. With better times after the Depression, old Model A Fords and similar cars were hauled out of lean-to garages or even a farm junkyard and restored to running order. A trip into town could then be done with ease, the whole family enjoying the ride.

At our home, an end-of-week cleaning up was required first of each of us, after an early supper. We all dressed in our Sunday best—Dad wore his suit and tie, Mother her hat and most fashionable dress—and away we went. It seemed we had only work garb or best wear: there were no in-between clothes.

At town the cars angle-parked against neat concrete sidewalks in the one-block business section of Main Street, filling up both sides. It was strictly a farmers' night out—every jalopy had its fine dusting of soil (or splattering of mud) from the country roads. The stores, meanwhile, seemed to us to display the wealth of the world. They stayed open till ten to accommodate their farm customers.

Since we usually got to town at half-past seven, there was no rush about buying the week's groceries or some needed hardware, for there were neighbors to greet (not seen since the previous Saturday night), gossip to exchange, and crop news to relate. "Did you get any rain on Thursday? The clouds seemed to be heading your way." "Did you bring along that recipe we talked about?" "How's that boy of yours doing after his accident?" These were the questions asked, each person adding his or her own bit of information. Eventually everyone wandered off, singly or in pairs, to one store or another.

The first thing I did was to walk up and down the two sides of the street where all the cars were parked, hoping to meet one of my school companions. Then the two of us would continue walking the same route for a few loops, each glad to have a chum along.

A side jaunt, half a block away, took us to the station to watch the evening train come in. A fair number of people often gathered there just to see the steam locomotive, whistling from afar, chugging with huge wheels and side rods up to the platform, hissing out a jet of white steam along the tracks, and billowing out its black plume of smoke. To watch this "iron horse" screech to a stop was, for us, a magnificent sight. We lolled about the platform, hands in our pockets, each feeling quite the man about town.

Then it was back downtown for another round of Main Street. If one of us—and there might be three of us boys by now—actually had something to buy, we wandered through the town's two hardware stores or drugstore, gaping at all the brand new merchandise. A boy with a whole nickel to spend pondered a while before he made his purchase, and a pooling of three nickels opened up all kinds of possibilities—air-rifle BB shot at a hardware store, a pulp western magazine at the drugstore, or three ice cream cones at one of the cafés.

Our parents, meanwhile, had finished their shopping, but the social aspect of small-town Saturday night was just getting underway. Country people, except courting couples, tended not to frequent cafés then—they could drink coffee at home. The farmwives sat two or three in a car, instead, and had a good visit. The men sat on the running boards of adjacent cars, or stood in front with a foot on a bumper, discussing world events and settling them with a satisfying finality.

Occasionally the evening's entertainment was taking in a movie at the local theatre. A lot of the movies were B Westerns (the best kind), and we became acquainted with Gene Autry, Roy Rogers, and the Sons of the Pioneers. They spoke to our world of down-to-earth values, for we were sons of the pioneers ourselves.

One movie I remember well was a dude-ranch Western-musical-comedy. We laughed as one of the characters tried to milk a cow by swinging her tail up and down like a pump handle. What appealed to me most, though, was the fine voice of star Dick Foran singing a new song (later a standard), "I'll Remember April," during a moonlit trail ride.

Our whole family also attended another memorable movie, Look Who's Laughing, for it featured the popular radio stars Fibber McGee and Molly. Seeing this middle-aged couple on screen (they were married in real life) was like seeing old friends—they looked just as we had envisioned them. To our delight, some of the other characters from their radio program also dropped by their movie home at 79 Wistful Vista—The Great Gildersleeve, Mrs. Uppington, and Harlow Wilcox. And to have Edgar Bergen and Charlie McCarthy, also of radio fame, there, too, as well as a very young Lucille Ball, was an extra bonus.

Leaving the darkened theatre, we entered the glitter of Main Street again, all the more aglitter now because night had finally come on; it was time to head for home. Back in our own yard, the car's headlights bored two beams through the darkness against the garage. Inside, we were in the dark as before, once the lights were switched off. Groping our way to the house, opening doors, reaching for a coal-oil lamp on its shelf, striking a match to light it—these restored us to a warmly lit kitchen.

We sat around the table, recounting news we had heard or describing a highlight or two from the movie we had seen. Mother put a going-to-bed snack and some coffee or milk before us. It was pleasant just to be home.

It seemed that our pattern of going to town would never end—that's how our life was. It seemed that my parents would always be there to go to town, as would the rest of us, happily ensconced in our Model A. The town would always be the same, its Main Street glittering, its stores flourishing. This was part of our world, our summer world, and we wished for no other. The war was over or ending, prosperous times were ahead, our mortgage was finally paid—how could things be better, or different?

Haydn Pearson, in another essay from *The New England Year*, sums up those days: "Those were good times in a boy's life. There was peace and family unity. One had a secure feeling …."

Dad's Winter Trips to Town

When Dad and Mother got married in 1918, they had no horse to drive the first winter so Dad walked the four miles of winding trail across fields to Rosthern each week. Mother stayed at home, keeping the fires burning and awaiting his return. He was gone until dark in those short winter days, and a coal-oil lamp shining in the window welcomed him back. But my recollection of the 1940s is of him going to town by horse and cutter.

Thursdays were chosen for his drive because the two weekly farm papers we received, *The Free Press Prairie Farmer* and *The Western Producer*, were in our post-office box that day and it was good to come home with some mail. Sometimes storms prevented his leaving so that two weeks might go by (once it was three weeks) without contact with the town world. Was there ever a quantity of mail and funny papers from the weeklies to look at joyfully then!

The day started with Dad taking Bruce in from the pasture and giving him an extra feed of oats in the barn (normally our livestock wintered outdoors). Bruce liked his freedom, but he knew what was coming and enjoyed prancing before the cutter as well.

The rest of us did our part, too, for the trip was not lightly undertaken. Mother had made up her grocery list, with not so much on it really, but it needed explaining. For example, if

McIntosh apples were not available, Dad should maybe see what other fruit the store had. Something fresh to eat was needed in wintertime—as much for the novelty of it, to break the monotony of the gray winter days, as for the nutrition. Also if Dad did buy apples, then he should get some cinnamon for making apple pies; if not, he should buy nutmeg instead, to flavor a pudding.

Meanwhile, Dad was eating a substantial early dinner of mostly non-store items: coffee with rich cream (from the cows he and Mother had milked that morning), fried chunky home-grown potatoes with cracklings (from a pig butchered that year), and brown bread and butter (he ground his own meal, and Mother churned the butter).

Now to assist in the final stages of leaving, one of us children harnessed Bruce in the barn, led him to the waiting brown cutter, and backed him between the shafts for hitching up. Bruce snorted and pumped his head up and down, anticipating the journey, his hoofs crunching in the snow.

My job was to get the fur robe out of the empty granary, where it had been stored since the last trip to town. I unfolded it and spread it over the seat, back, and sides of the cutter and over the floor. That way Dad would not have to sit directly on the cold boards. An old thick car robe, and as many blankets as the day's temperature dictated, completed the equipage.

Usually we stowed two additional items in the cutter: an oat bundle pushed under the seat for Bruce's snack while in town and the five-gallon can of cream to be delivered at the local creamery (if some of the cows had already freshened and were yielding enough milk), which would pay for the groceries.

Dad came out of the house in felt boots, two pairs of pants, flannel shirt, wool sweater, windbreaker, and thick fur coat, along with huge mitts and heavy cap. Although he could not rightfully make the statement of a similarly clothed, 1860s adventurer in our area, Walter B. Cheadle—"O! by Jove! I could hardly move"—he was not likely to get cold that day. Once seated and grasping the reins securely, he clucked twice with his tongue,

Bruce strained into the harness, and the cutter squealed into motion. A bit of sideways lurch swung the runners into line, starting Dad and Bruce on their way.

Bruce trotted out of the yard and onto the cross-country trail heading west. Willow clumps and aspen poplars in our pasture screened Dad from view before he left our farm, but three openings through the trees allowed us to glimpse horse and driver as they passed each point in turn and disappeared from sight.

Having gone along with Dad on occasion, I knew what the following trip was like. Bruce slowed to a walk. The muffled stamp of his hoofs on the snow, the swish of the runners, the creak of harness but emphasized the stillness of the winter day everywhere about—a white silence with only some rabbit tracks to tell of possible life and movement over the next rise. There were just slopes of grayish snow, edged at places with stands of bare trees: nothing astir in a cold world.

Then Bruce resumed his trot, and this world slipped by, gray-blue shadowings and frosty haze along the horizon. With the faster pace and more distance covered, the landscape showed that there was life about. The jackrabbit, its tracks seemingly caught up to it, stood erect, watching the horse and cutter from a distance, then went off in a series of toddling hops. A flock of gray partridges, sounding alarm notes, took sudden wing, fluttering noisily and then sailing in a graceful arch-winged curve to cover elsewhere.

Dad sat, snug in his robes, at peace with things. An elderly man by then, he was thankful he could enjoy this weekly adventure, this time with birds and animals of the wild, seen from his open-air cutter, with strong and dependable Bruce pulling it. The farm was a good place to be—he liked the freedom of the outdoors as well as Bruce—and going to town was always a prelude to coming back, doubling the pleasure of the drive through the countryside.

Bruce alternately trotted briskly and ambled along, and Dad felt the reins correspondingly tug urgently or go limp. So the journey proceeded—looping around bushes and crossing intervening fields. But on nearing town, Bruce's ears perked up, and he broke into a steady trot, the pace ever quickening. He was a show-off, and the rhythmic *clop-clop* of his hoofs on the trail dislodged circles of packed snow.

In town Dad hitched the horse to a rail on an empty lot off Main Street. On a cold day, he threw a blanket over Bruce while the horse munched on his oats. And on a really cold day, Dad left Bruce at a livery barn for a fee of twenty-five cents before beginning his errands to the grocery and hardware stores, post office, and maybe the drugstore.

By the time Dad had stowed his purchases safely in the cutter, Bruce had had a rest, and it was time to go home. The winter day would soon become grayer with the changing light at day's end, and both horse and driver were anxious to be on the road again.

If they started from the livery barn, there was always some trouble in getting away. Dogs from town—there were no pet bylaws then—tended to congregate about the stable to give the departing teams a harried send-off. So here was Bruce, already fidgety to be gone, flailing out sideways with his hoofs at a pack of yapping, jumping dogs, and Dad standing up in the cutter, trying to get the animals to disperse and Bruce to canter ahead. Finally the conveyance broke free from the pack, and a quick flap of the reins sent Bruce speeding down the trail, leaving the dogs to fall back one by one. It was like a scene from the Russian steppes (where my Dad was born) with a troika and sleigh outracing a wolf pack across the snowy plains.

Out in the open countryside once more, Bruce slowed down, but the way pointed homeward, and the stretches of trotting were longer now. On one previous occasion, with Mother along, the horse's fast pace had caused the cutter to tip over (one runner had caught on a hummock). The cutter swerved sharply and fell onto its side, spilling out both my parents and the box of groceries. Apples were rolling along the roadway, and Mother was convulsed in laughter. "Ansh," Dad had chided, "hold off laughing and pick up the apples." He was glad she had not been hurt.

Another time Dad found the entire road clogged with the afternoon's drifting snow, and in one hollow the drifts were several feet deep. Bruce plunged ahead, got stuck, waited a moment, then took a number of leaps, leaving the cutter to slither somehow over the drifts behind him. It was then that a harness trace tore, and progress was immediately stopped. As it happened, my skates were on the cutter, and their stout leather laces were used to improvise repairs. The cold was intense, and the work had to be done barehanded—there was no other way of tying the necessary knots linking harness to shaft with the looping laces. It was mainly strength of will that got numbed and fumbling fingers to complete the repairs.

On this day, though, there were no delays or mishaps. The road was good, and when the sky along the horizon began to grow dusk, Mother sent one of us to watch at the window. Others watched, too. Before long we saw horse and cutter through the opening in the trees at the border of our farm. "He's coming," we shouted.

Soon Dad appeared at the second opening, and we rushed to put on our rubbers, mitts, caps, and mackinaws in readiness. When he appeared at the opening nearest home, we scrambled outside and stood waiting in the yard. Bruce saw us from afar and put on a splendid burst of speed as Dad circled into the yard.

Now each of us had a job to do. An older brother unhitched the horse, led him to the barn, and tended him there. Another carried in the box of groceries, while I folded the heavy robes neatly and returned them to the granary.

When Dad saw that all was well, he walked to the house with the important mail, tied with store-string to make sure that none would be lost, clutched in his mitt. Perhaps he had got a little cold after all or maybe he was cramped from sitting so long. Anyway, the exclamation—"O! by Jove! I could hardly move"—was more applicable to him now as he entered the house.

There, Mother was examining the box of groceries to see which items were present and what substitutions had been made. Store-bought goods were nice to handle and put away in the pantry. Yes, everything was all right, even the McIntosh apples, and she gave Dad an approving look. Satisfied, Dad carried his bundle of papers into the living room.

It was no work for Mother now to whip up an apple pie and shove it into the oven of our big kitchen range. From there its sweet cinnamon smell would waft through the whole house as it baked for supper while we took care of the evening chores of milking and tending the livestock.

That evening, after the supper dishes were put away, everyone gathered about the living-room table to read of the week's news and activities at leisure. Again, a coal-oil lamp shone forth its warm yellow light as it had so many years earlier when Dad, as a newlywed, had returned from his walk to town.

While Dad read the papers for farm happenings and Mother looked at some new recipes or stories in the "women's pages," we children pored over the funny papers. There were *The Western Producer*'s "Katzenjammer Kids," Hans and Fritz, riding their ostriches and elephants on an exotic desert island. Equally exotic to us were the adventures of "King of the Royal Mounted"

in *The Free Press*, for while they occurred in Canada, often amid a wintry landscape like ours, his transportation was by dog team and ski-equipped airplane.

We were all happy to be together again at day's end, sharing our joys around a lamplit table. We were well content with Bruce and the cutter for our present travel, and just as glad each time Dad got back from his weekly winter trip to town.

X

GETTING AWAY

A Day at the River

The South Saskatchewan River was six miles east of our farm, at Gabriel's Crossing, where Gabriel Dumont had operated a ferry before the 1885 North-West Rebellion. In the early 1940s, our family spent many happy afternoons fishing there.

It was natural that the river should be important to us. My grandfather had at one time fished commercially, selling his catch in Rosthern; Dumont, granted amnesty for his part as Louis Riel's military leader in the resistance, was still living along its shores then. The river supplied a variety of fish—goldeye and chub, redhorse, sucker, burbot, and sturgeon. But more than a provider for our table, the river was a retreat, an escape from workaday life. At a time when little rain fell from the searing sky above the prairies, the sound of flowing water and the damp coolness of a shaded bank gave us another world.

A typical outing started with Dad coming in at noon after sitting on the disc all morning behind the plodding horses. He was dust-blackened and perspiring. "Ansh," he said, "let's go to the river." Farm work seemed so hopeless.

The preparations for the excursion were an important part of our total enjoyment. After dinner Mother immediately packed a lunch—a loaf of homemade bread, butter hauled out of the well, a quart sealer of saskatoon-and-rhubarb jam, perhaps some hard-boiled eggs, and a jug of black coffee. Our baskets of fishing tackle were stowed in the Bennett wagon, and we were ready to go. All we had to do was catch our fishing bait.

Pesky grasshoppers were only too plentiful in those days, and we caught them and slipped them into bottles stopped with grass. There was an art to catching them. They so blended with the parched grass that we saw them only after they had whirred away in flight before our feet. Then we had to note where one landed and approach cautiously, cupped hand held in readiness to imprison the insect before it flew up again. A quick slap of the hand upon the quarry—and upon a screen of grass! It was under the grass, but … ? Slowly moving our hand sideways, we tried to close our fingers on it, not always successfully. As a young boy, I would *crawl* toward a hiding grasshopper and spring at it, my legs flinging out backward as I came down on one hand with the grasshopper pinned beneath. Catching a bottle full of grasshoppers was a proud accomplishment before the fishing even started.

The hour-long drive to the river heightened our anticipation. Who would catch the first fish that day? Who would catch the most goldeyes? On a wagon a boy could walk about and work off some excitement. And the slow trip gave ample time to look at roadside flowers, gaillardias and brier roses, and to hear meadowlarks singing from fence posts.

Soon the blue hills across the river rose into view. As we began our winding descent among the sand hills on this side of the water, we stood on tiptoe to be the first to catch a glimpse of it through the trees below.

For most of the descent we followed a steep cut down the

side of a hill, the horses straining to hold the wagon back. Then we swung off along a narrow trail on a wooded terrace above the shore where the horses could trot freely. Willow, aspen, birch, and hazelnut branches scratched against the sides of the wagon, and we inside dodged overhanging limbs. At last we burst into a grassy clearing with the friendly river sparkling below.

Dad unhitched the horses and tied them to a tree about which they could graze. Mother set the lunch near the cool spring that flowed there. We children scrambled down the sandy bank. Should we fish on the stony shore to the left of the spring or on the curving stretch of sand on the other side?

Whatever our choice for the day, soon our board spools were bobbing like yo-yos as we unraveled our thick hand-lines from them. Once we had baited our lines and secured them to willow poles stuck into the muddy shore, we twirled them around our heads and flung them into the water; each willow pitched forward before stopping the sinker's flight. Line and sinker rolled with the current a short distance before lodging. The next time the willow bent forward, we knew we had a fish.

The afternoon's sport was watching someone else run to a line when a fish was biting, slipping in the mud in his haste or clattering among the stones and stubbing his toes. Others rushed to the spot to see the fish being pulled out, shouting instructions meanwhile: "Hey, it's a goldeye!" "Steady does it now." "Don't ease up."

The goldeye, the principal fish caught, was much given to aerial leaps, which added to the spectacle if not to some disappointment, for it might shake the hook. Often it got free in the shallow water just at shore. Then the fisherman jumped into the water, not caring about his shoes, and learned how slippery the fish really was. If landed, the fish was put into a gunny sack immersed in the water, with a large stone across the open end.

For a young boy, catching even a lowly chub was a thrill. These fish were nibblers, taking the bait off the hook many times without getting caught. By holding the line in my hand, instead of fastening it to a willow stick, I could feel the nibbles and try to set the hook. Sometimes an afternoon would pass by with a chub still uncaught. But meanwhile, holding onto my line, I had been communicating with the underwater world, attuned to the vibrations being sent along this cord that fixed me to nature. I could even feel a dragonfly landing on that part of the line above the water.

By late afternoon it was time for our picnic lunch. Sitting beside the stream, we could savor also the fresh outdoors. Henry David Thoreau said in a eulogy to wild apples that they should be eaten in the wind so that all the senses, and not just taste, were fed. To accompany our meal, we had the burbling sound of the stream, the moist scent of the river and the luxuriant growth along its shores, the firm feel of sand to sit upon, and the panoramic view of the flowing river before us with the opposite bank now in the warm light of departing day.

Our outing would soon end, but it was pleasant to sit a while in the cool of the evening and watch the shadows lengthen across the water. Always our parents made the first move to leave, for we children could have stayed forever, it seemed. Mother began gathering up the lunch; Dad started to clean the fish he had caught. We knew that we must clean ours, too. Still, we left our lines in the water, in hope of one last catch.

As we bent over the water's edge, working on the fish, ring-billed and California gulls began to circle above, calling to each other, dropping down to pick up entrails floating out with the current. Sometimes they would catch in midair some refuse thrown at them, and on one occasion I saw a California gull swallow a goldeye head whole. With these splendid scavengers around, the fishing site remained scrupulously clean.

Then we were on our way home, leaving the river valley behind. It was always a surprise to find on ascending the hills that we were back in the hot, sunlit world once more. There, fields continued to be parched, with dust thrown up in swirls by the wind. But by the time we reached home, the evening coolness surrounded us.

Quickly, there were chores to be done. The cows, waiting at the gate, were restless to be milked. Dad set about making a smudge while Mother fetched the pails. I walked across the pasture to our well to fill the cattle troughs with water. When I returned, the milking was finished. Mother went into the kitchen then while the rest of us saw to the other chores—separating the milk, feeding the calves and pigs.

When we got inside, the coal-oil lamp was lit and the table set. A final treat was still in store for us—eating the freshly fried fish and reminiscing about the highlights of that wonderful day.

Going to the Ex!

Since all of my country-school teachers had grown up on farms just like ours, they were not likely to pose that perennial back-to-school fall assignment: "What I Did in the Summer Holidays." In the aftermath of the Great Depression, farmers were paying off debts and were tied down to tending cows, pigs, and chickens because crops were so poor. If a teacher asked us where we had been on the holidays, we would have said, "Nowhere"; what had we done? "Nothing."

But in 1941 we *had* done something, and it came about in this manner. Our neighbors, who were better off than we and drove a car, had spent a few days at a northern lake. To do so, they had asked my parents to milk their cows in their absence, promising that in return they would take us to the Saskatoon Exhibition later that summer. So when the great day finally arrived, we were raring to go.

The sun was shining, as always, and there was not a cloud in the sky. We did our chores early that morning and walked the quarter-mile to our neighbors. We had already planned how we would all get into their car, a 1930 Model A Ford. (Our 1928 Model A stood unused in our garage because we still could not afford to drive it.)

The neighbor's car had two bucket seats in front and a bench seat in the back that could seat three at most. Though we were eight all told—four parents, two grown-up children, and two youngsters—we managed. The two fathers sat in front with the neighbor's youngster in between, sitting on the inside edges of the bucket seats. The two mothers sat in back, along with the grown-up neighbor's daughter. My brother Ted sat on a narrow plum box, set endwise between the front and back seats, while I, the youngest of the lot, either stood or sat on my mother's knee. "Ah-oo-ah," the Model A horn sounded, and off we went.

I do not remember much of the fifty-mile trip to the Saskatoon fairgrounds, but I am sure that we were pleased to get out and stretch cramped legs after a drive of an hour and a half. We would be on our feet for most of the rest of the day.

Our parents paid for our admission onto the grounds with the last of their money. From then on our entertainment would be strictly sightseeing. We had expected nothing else, and for unsophisticated farm children like us, just being at the Saskatoon Exhibition was a great experience.

The sense of smell, apparently, is one of our most primitive or basic senses; any sensations derived through it can remain with us through a lifetime. So it is for me now when I smell fried hamburger outdoors. Immediately I am wafted back to the exhibition midway of 1941. There were several food booths along it, dispensing not only hamburgers, with fatty, somewhat burned odors, but also steaming hotdogs and sugary confections. I recall, mixed with these smells, the heavy odor of wet sawdust.

And the smells trigger other sensations. I hear again the cries of barkers hawking their wares outside a brown tent and see most vividly in my mind's eye a beggar, with legs amputated at the knees, hobbling about one of the booths on his rubber-padded stumps. Even without going into any of the sideshows, this small farm boy was encountering a completely different world.

There were tents in which games of chance were held, the operator spinning a clacking wheel. What confidence these operators had, how forward they were, and how self-assured was their speech! I was used to farmers leaning against a fence, both looking straight ahead (never at each other), and discussing things with expressions like "maybe" and "I hope" and "we'll see" in their soft-spoken voices. Here at the exhibition, there were no "buts" or "ifs," just certainties. Throw a ball and win a prize. It was as simple as that.

I enjoyed watching some children my own age sitting in toy cars and driving into each other, bouncing off, and driving into somebody else. It did not occur to me that I might enjoy being in one of the cars, too. Similarly, I watched people eating candy floss, pink and fluffy. I did not know what it was called, and I did not know how it tasted. Again, it did not occur to me to ask my parents whether I might have some. But there was no need to ask either. I was awestruck enough by the sight of other people eating it.

What we ate were some boiled eggs and brown bread and black coffee, which we had brought along from home and could enjoy in the shade of the car on that hot day. It was a picnic for us, and we had seen so much already.

Finally we had to say goodbye to that exotic world, take up our cramped quarters in the Model A again, and make our return journey. It was a time to recount the adventures of the day, the sights seen and sounds heard. My brother was particularly excited and talkative: "Do you remember the … ?" "Did you see the … ?" "And what about the … ?" So ran his questions, and various ones of us chimed in with answers. I merely listened, happy to relive the events. Somewhere along the way I must have fallen asleep.

Sleep did not take away any of the memories, however. Next day, each incident was still vivid in my mind. And when school started in fall, I for once had something unique to say about my summer holidays, whether the teacher assigned us that topic or not.

A Car for a Lifetime

The 1928 Model A Ford Instruction Book, issued to each owner some seventy-five years ago, began: "In the New Ford, you will find each of [the] systems of the latest design and built in the best material. Every part has been made to serve you faithfully and well." Faithfully and well, indeed! Some present-day car fanciers maintain that, for its time, the Model A was the best car ever built. I was brought up with this car and came to know it almost as a member of our family. It was very much a part of our lives.

By 1928 farming had prospered just enough that my parents could buy the Model A. It was new that year, and Dad took delivery of the first one to be unloaded at the railway station in Rosthern. Costing $800, it would be his car for a lifetime.

Proudly he had walked about the vehicle. Painted a two-tone dark green and black, the car seemed for those days much brighter than the Model T in its staid solid black. The top rear corners of the body were no longer angular, and the front had a short awning above the windshield—both features contributing to a streamlined look—while there was nickeled trim about the radiator and on the headlamps. Dad reasoned that, all in all, that was about as far advanced as car design could go: "The corners are rounded off—what else can be done?" he asked Mother rhetorically.

Alas, there were farm debts to pay, and the next year the Great Depression started officially; there was no money to buy a licence, let alone gasoline, and the car stood idle year after year in the garage built for it. But it was not sold—in truth, could not be sold—for it represented better times that once had been and could be again.

So Dad drove the car for only three summers, 1928 to 1930, before he put it away. In that time it made one trip to Herbert in southwestern Saskatchewan's soon-to-be Dust Bowl, where my parents attended a church conference, and into the Meadow Lake country up north, where some local people had recently homesteaded. Apart from that, mostly it went to Rosthern for mail and groceries once a week, and to the South Saskatchewan River on the occasional Sunday for fishing. Then the car went into storage and stayed there for eleven years.

Having an almost new Model A safe in the garage, and the hope of driving it again, was what, I suppose, kept my dad and mother going as much as anything during the bleak Depression years. What literally kept them going was a team of horses and wagon.

The car did not stay continuously in the garage. Every summer it received an annual washing, something of a family ritual to be looked forward to each year. All of us took part, first checking the tires for pressure, then pushing the car backward from the garage, finally scrambling behind it to send it forward to our well. After a few minutes we had it going at a running clip, with my older brother running alongside the open door to try to steer it. The rest of us were his backseat drivers, and the activity took on a boisterous holiday atmosphere.

When we had stopped at the well and were standing about our vehicle, it already seemed that we had had a short journey and were now stretching our legs for a break from driving. "Well, we're here at last—nice trip!" one of us would say, looking about at the scenery. One summer Mother thought it would be nice to have a picnic lunch at the well once the car was washed. She made sandwiches and packed some cookies and brought them to us. You would have thought we were a bunch of tourists sitting on the running boards, munching a sandwich and drinking the refreshingly cold well water.

Thus the yearly ritual continued until 1942, the year of the first bumper crop since 1929. It must have been a special moment for Mother and Dad to drive in the Model A once more. We were now a liberated family, with a car to take us places. And in spite of the gas rationing of the last years of the Second World War, we could never use up all our ration coupons. We had been without a car for so long that it was hard to splurge and drive just anywhere, and there was little money to spend anyway with the farm still in debt. So drives were mainly to town on business or to the river for an afternoon's fishing, as they had been a decade before.

When I think back now, some of the situations involving our car travel seem odd by today's fast-paced standard. In one incident my sister, a new teacher, was looking for a boarding place to start her term in a neighboring school district. My brother offered to drive her about from farmyard to farmyard, making inquiries. I went along for the ride. We were directed from one house to another and spent the whole afternoon making the rounds. When we got home, the odometer registered twenty miles traveled! What would our parents say? (They did not say anything.) On a different occasion this same brother drove off to town, without consulting anybody, because he was expecting mail at the post office. To make a four-mile trip just for one letter seemed an unheard-of extravagance. (That time my parents did say something.)

I remember two longer trips. In one we were all sitting in the car, impatient to be off, all of us, that is, except Dad. Because of the destination—Wakaw Lake, twenty-eight miles distant—he felt it necessary to make a last-minute check of the car: water in the radiator, gasoline in the tank, water in the battery (accessed by way of a plate-metal cover in the floorboards), oil in the crankcase, and air in the tires. After each tire had been suitably kicked, we were ready to go.

Meanwhile a trip to Prince Albert, fifty miles away, was just too distant for a non-stop drive. Of course, shimmying front wheels (worn kingpins) and a loose-gravel highway made things more tiresome. Halfway there, in the Nisbet Provincial Forest, we stopped to rest, stretch our legs, and walk about the car. Mother, with her Kodak Junior bellows camera, took a picture of us lined up beside the Model A.

Then came 1944, a memorable year in our family, for that year Dad and Mother paid the last installment on the debt that they owed on the farm. The sandy quarter-section of land on which they had worked so unsparingly was finally theirs, and they deserved a real holiday, an extended trip in the Model A. We children would look after the chores at home.

The trip proceeded along country roads to Fish Creek Ferry, nine miles southeast and still in operation in the 1940s, then south to the Manitou Beach resort at Watrous, through the Qu'Appelle Valley at Lumsden, and on to Regina and Moose Jaw, finally looping homeward along Buffalo Pound Lake to Saskatoon and Rosthern. On the gravel highways the Model A purred ahead at a speed of twenty miles an hour, with Mother urging Dad to watch the road and not drive too fast.

Mother had packed meals to be eaten en route: a large baked ham, buns and butter, three rhubarb pies, and four quarts of black coffee. The last mortgage payment left no money for restaurant meals. Nights were spent sleeping beside the car on a blanket under the stars.

At Regina, the operator of the tourist camp, where my parents had already stayed one night, asked wonderingly, "How come you're sleeping on the ground here?"

Mother quickly explained the situation—why they were on vacation.

"Do you call this a holiday?" the operator asked, amazed.

"Yes," my mother replied, unabashed, looking at the car, "the best one we ever had."

Two days later, my parents were home again, safe and sound, the reliable car having made a five-hundred-mile round trip for its happy owners. "Ah-oo-ah," the horn sounded, as they proudly drove into the yard. The car was once more under roof in its old garage, while Mother and Dad had a bed to sleep in at home, sweet home.

City attractions and faraway scenes were fine, but this car for a lifetime was best used helping with daily activities on and about the farm. The Model A was really very serviceable in this regard. The right front seat folded down and tipped underneath the dash, providing ample room for sliding the five-gallon can of cream into the back to haul to the creamery.

When our yard well went dry in late summer, this same cream can was used to haul water from our livestock well. I was not of driving age, but the job was given to me since the route was solely on our farm. It was while steering the Model A around willow clumps, through an opening in a poplar bluff, and over a hilly hayfield—all the while following a cow path to the well—that I learned to drive. Later, when I got my licence, it was no trick for me to take the Model A, with wagon in tow, across stubble fields to where the grain was threshed, then on to town and up the elevator ramp with a load of wheat. It was no trick for the sturdy little car either.

When I attended town school for grade twelve, with the cold weather of November and December, I ceased bicycling into town, and Dad drove me to school each morning in the Model A. And every day after school he waited in the unheated car, ready to take off the robe thrown over the radiator, to take me home. But at Christmas my father died of a heart attack—in his Model A. Mother was beside him, with Ernie at the wheel, driving to the hospital in Rosthern.

When the country roads opened in May after a horrendous winter of deep snow, I drove to school alone. Only Mother and I were left on the farm now, and I became the sole driver of the car.

A year later I began teaching in a rural school at Wingard near historic Fort Carlton, and the Model A was my chief means of transportation. It took me over the thirty miles of strange winding roads to apply for the school—I had not yet turned nineteen—and later that fall took me back to the farm for weekends. The area was heavily wooded, with many cherry and berry bushes, and the roadways were corridors through textured autumn foliage—crimson, russet, and yellow—with some trees almost touching overhead.

A teacherage erected on the schoolyard in late fall became my residence for the two years I taught in the district, and my mother lived with me. The car now stood outside nearby, no longer under roof.

Two episodes from those days involving the Model A stand out. One occurred in February, following a month of near record-breaking cold. It was easy to get a little cabin fever sometimes between Christmas and Easter, with never-ending winter and the steady routine of teaching beginning to tell on the nerves. There were always fires to be made in the dark of early morning (in teacherage and school), wood to be split, and snow to be re-banked against the walls for insulation (and carried inside for water). By the end of February I realized we needed a mid-term break of sorts.

The urge came to me after one school day to start up the car and drive the twenty-five miles to Rosthern to take in an evening movie. Nowadays, winter car travel is commonplace, but over the farm roads we had then, most rural winter travel was done by bobsleigh and cutter, certainly not by older-vintage car without heat, let alone an engine-block heater. I set a bucket of water and antifreeze on the kitchen range to warm, poured that into the radiator, then resorted to the crank to get the engine going. It caught, and Mother and I, with a supply of blankets, got into the car and were off.

We reached Rosthern without mishap, saw Gene Kelly singing and dancing with *joie de vivre* on the sunny streets of Paris, then drove home, huddled under our robes, scraping the windshield and staring vigilantly ahead along the beam of light from the car's headlamps. We did not wish to lurch off the narrow track of the snowy road and be stranded for the night. Nothing untoward happened, and I got less than a full night's sleep afterward, but with what fresh enthusiasm I resumed teaching the next day and continued so for the rest of the winter.

The other episode occurred at Easter, the long winter finally over and a week's holidays just beginning. But how to get away for a real break? The roads were in the worst possible condition, deep snowdrifts covering some sheltered sections and muddy quagmires in the open spots. A school trustee kindly offered to follow us with his team and wagon to pull the car through those spots where we might get stuck. (The first several miles were the worst until the trail connected with a higher grade.) I put chains on the car's back tires, and off we went.

First came a stretch of impossible undulating snowdrifts. Here previous teams had driven off the road and looped across an open field. So did I. But the field was half-thawed, and the back wheels immediately sank up to their axles. Although the field was level, I seemed to be continuously driving uphill because of the tilt of the car. Luckily, at axle depth, the wheels got traction on the frozen substratum, and we took off. The trustee paused with his team behind us and did not bother following any farther. He figured if we could proceed through that morass, we would be all right in the rest of the mud holes. And we were. The Model A was always, in racehorse terminology, a good "mudder."

I continued to drive the car until the late 1950s. In the summer of 1953, the engine had been completely overhauled and the car repainted in its original colors. It might have been 1928 all over again with a "new" Model A standing in our farmyard.

But times were slowly a-changing. I took a summer job in the city in 1955, after a winter's university attendance, and so did not buy a car licence that year. The car stood idle in its garage as it had done for so many years in the past and would soon do again, permanently. The last car licence I bought for it was for 1957. The vehicle still performed admirably, and I drove it all that summer as well as in April of 1958 before the licence expired.

It was now thirty years since my father had bought the car, and there I was, about to store it in the farm garage, after 50,000 miles of faithful service. So it would stand for another thirty years, until the late 1980s, when I had it towed to a new garage for safekeeping.

All my memories of it came to mind as I climbed into the car and gripped the red steering wheel for the last time in preparation for towing. Soon we were clipping along, and for a moment I felt like a young man again, driving to my first school, beginning life's great adventure, doing so fittingly in our family Model A, a car for a lifetime.

XI

GROWING UP

My Summer of '42

In my boyhood, the summer of 1942 was unique for our family. The year had started the same as other years, my dad having put in fifty acres of wheat as well as some oats for feed as he always did.

So we were looking for rain again once the crop was seeded. Whenever some thunderheads showed in the west, my brother Ernie would stand just inside the summer kitchen, squinting through the crack where the door was hinged, trying to gauge which way the clouds were moving. "They're going to come over," he usually said. This he had said in other years, too, but clouds in a thundershower circle and crisscross, and the rains had generally swung off to the north or to the south, bypassing our farm. I know now that this was partly the illusion of perspective because the sky offers such a panoramic view. But the clouds did tend to swing along a shower belt to the northwest. As a result, the farmers there had a chance to brag about their fifteen-bushel crops while the rest of us looked at our shriveled stands.

The crop was not yet up when one evening, I remember, we had just returned from visiting our neighbors. A huge electrical storm was building up in the west and now covered half the sky. The heavy clouds were bluish black underneath, plumped out as if a drum for the thunder that rumbled all the while. The whole cloud mass churned around. There could be no doubt that it would come over our farm this time.

My dad was the last to go inside after the horses were unhitched. He stayed standing in the middle of the yard, watching the storm come on. Then I saw him raise his arms diagonally above his shoulders, while staring up at the clouds. The thunder continued to roar menacingly. What was he trying to do anyway? Appeal to the rain gods to release their blessings upon his fields? Defy the elements that had long thwarted his efforts? Or was his gesture sheer exhilaration caused by the veering of winds and the kaleidoscope of milling clouds? He just stood there. The whole thing seemed a little mysterious and frightening to an eight-year-old boy; it was a scene I would not forget. Whatever Dad's purpose, my mother ran out to him, telling him to come in before he was struck by a bolt of lightning. The thunder clapped and rumbled; lightning forked to the horizon.

And it rained! At first a few felty drops, then a steady patter that sizzled like cracklings in a frying pan. We looked out the windows and saw the water "steaming" from the barn roof and puddles forming in the lane and before the summer kitchen. "Ansh, it's raining," Dad said to Mother, as if the event needed verbalizing.

After a few days there was a green sheen over our fields as the seedlings bent upright in neat rows through crumbs of earth. Mother and Dad walked over the land looking at the crop. Dad was a mild bald-headed man, partly deaf and fifteen years older than Mother, she a marked contrast—a stout, quick, little woman. Yet there they were, strolling through the greening fields, hand in hand like newlyweds, something they did every spring. But in '42 the land had for once got a soaking, and the prospects looked good. The pump had been primed, and maybe it would rain some more. A lot of rain was needed in the growing season.

There was always enough food on the farm, even during the Depression, but it's funny how one got a craving for something special to eat that was store bought. That's why one trip to town that year stands out in my memory. We children and Mother were sitting on the bench in our wagon, stopping at the creamery, while Dad held the horses' reins. We were waiting for our cream to be graded and for our check to be made out so that we could buy groceries.

Everyone was impatient. Dad always wanted to get home from town as soon as possible. That was why he had a home—to be there. The rest of us wanted to go home, too. Town was not a bad place to go to, but it was a better place to come from. One-eyed Beauty and old Tom were shaking their heads at the flies, standing each with a hind leg drawn forward, then shifting their weight to a different three legs.

Mother sensed that a treat would be nice on getting home, and the crop, five inches high by now, looked good. She had the clerk put a chocolate bar into our grocery box—something she was to repeat several times that summer as the crop steadily kept growing. A crop on the field wasn't any money in the pocket yet, but one could be a little extravagant at such times.

When we got home, Mother placed the chocolate bar in the center of the kitchen table and took the butcher knife from the drawer. Then she opened the bar's wrapper and cut the chocolate into six pieces, one for each of us. Mother could divide up any treats or desserts so evenly that it was impossible to find one portion larger than the others. No matter how hard we children looked—and this was one of those round lumpy bars with nuts in it—we could see that no one would get the advantage of any other. I think Mother was pleased with her skill in this regard.

There were several other pleasant things to recall about that memorable summer—before the sort of family tribunal at the end of it and my own brief personal disgrace. I suppose my discomfiture then only helped to make vivid in my mind the wonderful things that happened throughout the season.

One of those things was Dad's finding a little jar on walking through an alley in town during another trip there. It looked somewhat like a glass that one drinks out of today, but it had a friction top that was a little rusty—perhaps the jar had once been filled with jelly. Here was a prize to take home. Farmwives then hardly bought anything that came in jars—it's hard to imagine now—and Mother was as pleased with it as though she had received an unexpected gift. She had of course her quart jars, for canning saskatoon berries, and her two-quart jars, for filling with highbush-cranberry jam, but this new container was such a dear little jar! She scoured the top and gave the glass a good polishing. When friends came over, she asked them, "Now, what do you think I should put in it?"

It's surprising how well the wild fruit, the saskatoons and cranberries, did grow in those dry years. And when more rain came in '42, the berries were as luscious as you could hope for. There was a thick stand of saskatoon bushes just east of us on a place we called the berry farm, and during that summer particularly, starting in late June, the poorer townspeople walked out the half-dozen miles to pick their own berries. Usually there was a mother leading a troop of children—some her own, some the hangers-on from the town streets, now out for a lark. She'd be pulling a child's wagon, in which the youngest in the family sat, surrounded by empty lard and syrup pails.

Dad assumed that these berry pickers would come up the trail across his farm, but he didn't like them taking shortcuts across his wheat fields. In other years he might have hesitated saying something, but in 1942 nothing had damaged the crop yet—a shower had come along whenever needed—and the wheat was burgeoning up already into the shot-blade. Raising a crop was serious business to him (a fact brought home to me later that fall) and his life's work, which he didn't want others to take lightly. And so he tried to head the berry pickers off at the pass, explaining to them the damage they were doing. But it was hard in those days to convince some people that farmland was not public property. Some of them were nasty and foul-mouthed—even in front of their children.

We had other visitors that summer who tried to be obliging. They were representatives of a farm weekly that was trying to hold on to its advertising by keeping up a large subscribers' list. Two city men had come out in an old Ford with a chicken crate wired to its back bumper. They were driving from farm to farm, collecting fowl where farmers had no money for subscriptions.

It was a sight to watch these two perform. They descended on the chicken yard and ran and leaped after their quarry. The hens had always roamed freely about, running after grasshoppers, so they gave the men quite a chase. Coattails flew out, and shirttails too, as the men, unacquainted with farm animals, dashed about, puffing and yelling directions, while the chickens squawked and took wing. Mother stood in the doorway watching, exulting in the spectacle, her stout body convulsed in laughter.

It was easy to laugh in '42. The concealed head of grain pushing up in each wheat stem was broad and long, able to nurture many kernels. When these magnificent heads pushed past the shot-blade, the whole field took on a kind of braided look, like a thick rug. We children were as happy as our parents. It seemed as though nothing could go wrong. By August the crop had a sort of yellowy-green look, its own kind of blush that made it all the more appealing. It swayed slightly, the wind teasing its surface, sending waves rippling across it to race with the shadows flung from the careering clouds above.

And so the summer passed. The rains had come plentifully in the growing season; now the needed warm days were ripening the stand. It looked as though the threat of hail was over and rust prevented. Sawflies were never a problem for us, and as for grasshoppers—the spring had been too wet for them. It had been no fun in the previous dry years, driving along the fields with a wagon box full of moist poisoned sawdust, flipping the mixture out with an old shingle, and hoping the pesky grasshoppers would find it more appetizing than the fresh green seedlings. There was only one thing that could still get the crop, and that was one of those early-August frosts. Then you could walk out a few days later to be met by a sickening sour smell and know that the greenish-white kernels in every head of grain had shriveled up along with the income for the year.

How shall I say it? If this were an ordinary story, and not about 1942, you'd think that one of those misfortunes had come about, or something else unforeseen, and you'd find our family standing in the ruined crop, having to take hope in the fact that there would be another year.

But nothing did happen. The fields yellowed up nicely, and the kernels inside each head turned a lovely orange red, so plump and hard you could scarcely bite them. We cut the crop and stooked it, hauled it home by hayrack and threshed it, and got it into the bin dry. The whole family pitched in till the work was done.

It was after the wheat was safely stored in the granary that I learned something about growing up. I had turned nine but I was still very much an active boy who liked to play outdoor games and enjoy himself. Only there wasn't too much of that kind of thing to do, particularly by myself, since my two brothers and sister were quite a bit older than I was. I couldn't very happily play ball by myself; nor could I go swimming—the sloughs had no water in those days, not even that year.

Then one Sunday I was left alone—the others had gone visiting—and my cousin Jim from the next farm came over. He was an active boy like me, and we knocked out flies for a while, then played a two-man scrub, using the granary as a backstop.

It was one of those very warm early-fall days. We grew tired after a time, hot and sweaty, and I undertook to show my cousin the large pile of wheat in our granary. I had helped to shovel it in and was rather proud of the result.

My, that wheat looked cool and inviting! Before we knew it, we were both inside, out of the burning sun, and cavorting on top of the grain. When our shoes filled up, we kicked them off and continued our sport. We shoved some of the wheat into separate piles as though we were playing with sand on a beach, then waded through them. We thrust our arms into the resisting mass, coming up with handfuls of grain, which we flung about us. It was then that we got the idea of trying to "swim" on the surface. The wheat now got into our hair and our pockets. The uniqueness of the experience added to our fun.

But next morning I knew something was wrong as soon as I came in after breakfast. Mother turned around from the kitchen table and looked at me with a set expression. Ernie gave me the once-over with that "Ah-hah!" look of his. Ted just stared at me rather blankly.

Here was a kind of family tribunal coming up, with me as the main attraction. I could hear my sister, busy with something in the other room, feeling herself above my immature goings-on. My father wasn't present either, not because he was partly deaf but because it wasn't in his nature to chastise his children.

But Mother was aware of his disapproval of something I had done, and she felt called upon to speak about the matter. She was never one to beat about the bush. "Were you playing in the wheat yesterday?" she asked.

She spoke as kindly as she could, but that only made me feel more empty. Was it so wrong to play in the wheat, I wondered. I looked at my two brothers, but their expressions hadn't changed, and I could find no comfort there.

"If you tell the truth right away, we won't do anything," Mother said. Her expression hadn't changed either.

It was only with these last words that I began to realize the enormity of what I had done, but the full impact I couldn't know till later in life when I was older.

I had committed what at that time was a sacrilege to a farmer. Wheat wasn't something you played with. It was your livelihood and you respected it. You cherished it in the palm of your hand after it was harvested and you might shuffle it with your thumb as you examined it or even bite it to determine its grade, but you didn't play in it. I might have learned something from Dad's encounter with the berry pickers who trampled down his crop—I should have known what his feelings were.

I admitted my guilt as quickly as I could and retreated sheepishly outside. Tribunals in our family never lasted long and were soon forgotten. I thought of my disgrace for a few days, it's true, and I felt rather embarrassed the first time I saw Dad after that. But he never said anything, and he was too gentle ever to hold it against me.

Maybe this story is really a kind of atonement for playing in the wheat that day. But I don't want to make too much of that either. As I've been saying all along, the ending to that summer really wasn't so bad. I learned something about life, and something about respect and dignity.

The Cowboy Life

In my childhood it was almost every prairie boy's dream to be a cowboy—and to be one immediately in those golden days of imaginative youth. I do not mean a *cow boy*, for I was that already—herding our livestock to the well and watering them each day. One summer I was even in charge of two picketed calves, changing their grazing "range" every few days and carrying pails of water to them individually. No, I mean a real cowboy, a man of the West, someone who sat tall in the saddle, rode herd on thousands of cattle, and ate his meals at a campfire on the trail or else from the back of a chuckwagon.

In reflection, I know that the appeal of the cowboy life back then was something more than mere adventure or the freedom of outdoor living. Our young minds and hearts grasped something there we could not articulate, something to do with man's history, his vitality and longings of the soul. Perhaps what Jack Shaefer—author of the classic *Shane* (1949)—says elsewhere best delineates the attraction. The cowboy's story, he writes,

> represents the American version of the ever appealing oldest of man's legends about himself, that sun-god hero, the all-conquering valiant who strides through dangers undaunted, righting wrongs, defeating villains, rescuing the fair and the weak and the helpless—and ...

does [so] in terms of the common man, the derring-do of democracy, depicting ordinary everyday man, not armored knights or plumed fancy-sword gentlemen, the products of aristocratic caste systems, but ordinary men who might be you or me.

(Out West: A Western Omnibus, London:
Andre Deutsch, 1959)

Further, the cowboy lives out his role in "the bigness of vast rolling treeless plains and of mountains ... that opens outward, that beckons onward, that feeds the imagination with visions of unlimited possibilities." His is a "healthy, forward-facing attitude toward life."

So I was a cowboy in my heart and mind, an ordinary individual and defender of the right, at home in the great outdoors, alive to my surroundings, and forward-looking. The world lay ahead of me.

Being a "cowboy" affected my work, the everyday chores I had to do, from chopping wood to gathering eggs, for I performed them with a self-reliance that made my parents proud, they not knowing of my new-found sense of honor, my code of the West. I was nothing daunted by whatever tasks fell to me. Each presented "visions of unlimited possibilities." Carrying in wood was a replenishing of the "campfire" in the kitchen range (with Mother as camp cook). Collecting eggs was a scrounging for food in a "vast ... treeless plain."

Of all my activities, however, being a cowboy most affected my play. For several months on end I walked about with a gun at my hip. It was a wooden revolver of my own carving (with a handle wrapped in hockey-stick tape) fitted into a black denim holster. The latter I asked my mother to sew for me, and she added a wide belt to which she had stitched a row of spent cartridges from somebody's .32-caliber rifle.

My outfit included a high round-topped farmer's straw hat, which I had soaked in water and reshaped to flatten the crown, to give it a Spanish aspect. (Spaniards, after all, were the first North American cowboys.) To this end, too, I had added a wide silk band and bent up the brim all around. I wore a colored handkerchief about my neck as a bandana and one of Dad's old vests over my regular shirt *and* pants. The vest, of course, was too big for me and hung much below the belt line of my usual trousers.

Sometimes, for show, I wore my sister's trim rubber boots under the pant legs. That footwear, I felt, had the appearance of a real cowboy boot that would fit well in a stirrup—if only I had had a saddle and, more importantly, a horse.

Dad supplied the final item of my outfit: a rope. It was a new one and, full of twists, would not coil smoothly. I remember soaking it in a tub of water and then circling it between two posts to take the kinks out. Then an uncle spliced it around a grooved brass eye I had found among some old junk to make a genuine lariat or lasso. I used this for letting myself down from the barn loft, where I sometimes slept as though I were a hired hand.

The Spanish words "lasso" and "lariat" had a nice Western sound to my ear, and, dressed in my assembled outfit, I used them *pronto* on all occasions. I also bolstered my vocabulary with Spanish terms like *remuda, arroyo,* and *sombrero* and particularly liked the names for kinds of horses: *pinto* and *palomino.*

When one of my cousins, another "cowboy," came to visit, we would ride the range together, running about like loping horses, playing cowboys and rustlers among the willow clumps of our pasture, our log smokehouse being the guardroom or jail for the lawbreakers. We practiced lassoing fence posts, drawing guns from holsters, and rounding up dogies. *Whoopie Ti Yi Yo!*

From where did we learn about the Western derring-do life? From where did the cowboy influence come in those pre-television days? Certainly our reading was a source. Almost every newspaper, in its wad of weekly funny papers, carried a Western. *The Lone Ranger,* created by Fran Striker and drawn during most of its long forty-plus-year history by Charles Flanders, was one of the most popular. Starting as a radio serial, which we listened to as well (and so were introduced to classical music with the strains of Rossini's "William Tell Overture"), the story went back to 1933, my birth year, and became a comic strip about the time I started school and learned to read. Here in the illustrations was the valiant hero, righting wrongs and defeating villains. The ranger's deep radio voice and pictured masked identity but added to his appeal.

Red Ryder, the title character of another Western strip, was an ordinary, everyday, working cowboy whose sense of justice led him into all sorts of incidents where his self-reliance was called upon. Fred Harmon, who created the strip in 1938 (the year that *The Lone Ranger* became a funny paper), drew the desert plains and mountain locale authentically, giving a real feel of the West to his readers.

There were books, too, that prompted my Western leanings. I read both Mary O'Hara's *My Friend Flicka* (1941) and its sequel, *Thunderhead* (1943). "Thunderhead"—the term given to a mushrooming cloud, dynamic, powerful, and portending storm (and a term new to me)—was an apt name for the title white horse, whose great energy young Ken McLaughlin tried unsuccessfully to harness. Yet Ken's vision, surely, was "Western," and the white horse, as a symbol of the *Wild* West, was something healthy and freedom-loving to glory in. "In Wildness is the preservation of the World," wrote naturalist-philosopher Henry David Thoreau,

and he equated wildness with west-ness.

Will James's *Smoky* (1927) depicted another wild horse, a smoke-colored pony. Through a series of incidents—the horse is trained to be a cattle horse, then, after being stolen and ill treated, it reverts to wildness again, only to be reclaimed and subdued once more by its original owner—James gave an unsentimental description of the West, replete with cowboy lingo (and Spanish terminology). It was a joy to read his colorful account, which added so much to my own idea of being a true cowboy.

Then there were the pulp Westerns, thick compilations of cowboy yarns, which could be bought at drugstore newsstands for twenty-five cents. I read only two, but excitedly re-read them several times. On one occasion I recall going into town by bicycle—would it have been by horseback!—to buy some needed grocery item for Mother (the rest of the family was busy with field work). I was given an extra quarter and splurged on a pulp Western to read when I got home.

Some forty years later I wondered whether my boyish excitement on reading such "literature" was simply a mark of immaturity. Then, in an antique shop, I came across a Street & Smith's *Wild West Weekly* of 1933 with an original selling price of fifteen cents. I eagerly bought the magazine, liking the feel of the newsprint pages. On reading it, I was surprised at how literate the stories were—told directly in clear prose. After that I was not sorry that pulp Westerns had been a small part of my growing up, influencing my wish to be a cowboy.

Movies were another influence, however few I saw in our small-town theater. They were invariably black and white B Westerns, where the characters tended also to be black or white, bad or good. And yet this seeming lack of complexity in characterization was not wholly unsuitable for a world in which an undaunted "hero" defeated scheming "villains." We knew what good and bad were and liked to see the former quality in our heroes and the latter in our villains. How else could they be heroes or villains?

But there was a degree of complexity, too. In one movie I recall, the protagonist worked to make his fortune (honestly) at his gold diggings. The more he made, the more he became seduced by his wealth until at the end, in a kind of Tolstoyan twist ("How Much Land Does a Man Need?"), he wandered a-thirst over the wide western desert, seeking ever more wealth, desperately clutching the gold he already had, and succumbing at last to the bigness of the land and his own greed. He had lost a "healthy" attitude toward life.

A final influence was the popular music of the late 1930s and 1940s. Serials like *The Lone Ranger* were not the only things Western heard on radio sets in those years. Some of the music, even songs on the "Hit Parade," had a distinctly Western flavor. I am not referring to the kind of music that, sixty years later, is called country and western. There is really little "Western" about the modern brand: its roots are "hillbilly," coming out of the back-woods of Tennessee and nearby states.

The true Western music originated in cattle country, where cowboys worked, with pieces like "Home on the Range" and "Red River Valley," both folk songs whose authorship is unknown. We sang them lustily (or poignantly) in grade school, really longing for a home where buffalo roamed and deer and antelope played. Similarly, the hauntingly beautiful "Colorado Trail" and "Doney Gal" date back to early Western days.

The tunesmiths of that time realized there was still a longing for the days of the Old West, still a desire in adults, as well as boys, to be a cowboy. They responded with their own modern, hauntingly beautiful counterparts to the old ballads, such songs as "Twilight on the Trail," "There's a Gold Mine in the Sky," and "The Last Round-Up." Some others, although in the novelty vein, told us where our hearts really were: "I'm an Old Cow-hand" and "In My Adobe Hacienda." Still others echoed the Spanish flavor that I loved: "Lonely Rose of Mexico" (hauntingly beautiful again), "Mexicali Rose," and "South of the Border."

Two musical groups of the time had much to do with highlighting the cowboy life for me. In 1942 the Swing and Sway dance band of Sammy Kaye made a recording of a slow ballad, "Where the Mountains Meet the Sky," sung by vocalist Billy Williams. It is a farewell song in which a cowboy is heading for the far horizon ("where the mountains meet the sky") after saying "so long" to his parents and telling his sister not to cry. The words and music complement each other well, and I was always greatly taken by the song. Years later, when thumbing through an old folio, I discovered that Williams, a Texan, had in fact written the piece. He had also just a bit of a Western touch to his singing, and so, backed by the Kaye Orchestra and Choir, rendered the selection as nobody else could.

Kaye had Williams sing other Western songs with the band, such as "Don't Fence Me In" and one of my personal favorites, "Along the Navajo Trail" (also backed by the very fine band-as-choir, with its college-glee-club sound). Another splendidly arranged Kaye recording that I especially liked, but with another vocalist, was "Along the Santa Fe Trail." The titles of these tunes already say something about the atmosphere conveyed.

The second musical group was the Sons of the Pioneers. Roy Rogers, one of the three founding members of these singers of close harmony, would later appear in all of the media depicting cowboys in my boyhood. Though he soon left the group to star in films, he retained close ties with the Pioneers, who made several cameo appearances with him.

The two other charter members of the group were Bob Nolan and Tim Spencer, both accomplished composers. Nolan and/or Spencer wrote many of the group's hit recordings. Who does not know Nolan's "Cool Water" or "Tumbling Tumbleweeds," perhaps thinking they are part of the folk song tradition because the songs have been so closely identified with the West? My favorite Pioneers recording is still "Blue Prairie," composed by Nolan and Spencer. It speaks of "the night wind fallin'" and "a night bird callin'"—all part of evening descending on the bigness of the treeless plains. The excellent bass harmony provides a "blue" undertone to the whole scene.

What with such fine Western music heard on the radio at any time—along with Western funnies in farm weeklies, good Western books and magazines obtained from the newsstand or school or the town library (or borrowed from an aunt), and thrilling Western movies seen occasionally at the Saturday night theater—it is no wonder that I wanted to be a cowboy.

And in a sense I was. The idea filled my thoughts by day and my dreams by night. It colored my actions and enhanced my world. I indeed lived in a world "that open[ed] outward, beckon[ed] onward, that fe[d] the imagination with visions of unlimited possibilities."

$\mathcal{S}hoes$

My mother once told me of her delight in being promised new shoes by her father, then climbing up the lean-to of their farm-house and sitting there all afternoon, waiting and watching for him to come home from town, by buggy, five miles away. When he finally came into view, she climbed down to wait beside the road. What he brought was a pair of black shoes: ankle-high, laced, and double-toed. Not Cinderella's slippers, but she could hardly wait to rush inside the house to try them on.

For me, the most memorable shoes I received as a boy were not new but second-hand. My dad and I were out in the field, stooking the crop just cut by our binder. We rested for a while in the heat of the afternoon, slumped down in the scant shade of a stook, drinking from a jug of water we had secreted there when we started.

My feet were blistered that day—I had not put on any socks—and Dad took off his own stockings for me, saying that his shoes were really too tight for him to wear with stockings. His were good workboots, and like Mother's early ones, ankle-high, laced, and double-toed. But because they were just a pinch too small, he wondered whether I could wear them next time.

Well, I certainly could (with a pair of heavy wool socks), and I continued to wear them all that fall to school. I was not overly concerned with the maxim that you cannot put the same shoe on every foot. For me, Dad's boots had the weight and feel of hard work (that I had to do) and were a badge of my coming of age. I could not only walk a mile—really, many miles (we lived two miles from school)—in someone else's shoes, but I could feel that I was taking a giant step toward full membership in the adult world.

Most boys then wore running shoes. They were not the jogging wear of today (with stitched leather uppers, cushioned insoles, and padded tongues) but plain brown runners made of cloth melded into rubber soles and toes. These were light on the feet, and, laced up tight, felt like no shoes at all. They were good for scampering about, climbing trees, and leaping over fences.

Their one disadvantage was that the rubber-and-cloth combination stifled the feet, making them very hot. Low runners were better than the ankle-high variety in this regard, but they had their own separate failing. Because the roads we trod then were so dry from the continued droughts, we sank into loose sand for an inch or so with every step. Some sand always flipped upward as we lifted our feet, only to fall into our shoes.

In a few days a layer of packed ground covered the insole and had to be scraped out with an old knife blade between wearings, for we never had more than one pair of shoes at a time. That we had such a knife set aside just for this purpose says a lot about how dry things really were. We were indeed, according to Helen Gray Cone, "Rusty and dusty of hat and shoe" after every walk.

We also walked barefoot on occasion—when a boy is "glad in every toe" and "grass is cool between each toe" (Rachel Field, "Barefoot Days"). Doing so was all right on our front yard, but I was not really "The Barefoot Boy" of John Greenleaf Whittier's poem. Unlike a cousin who did spend most of his summer holidays unshod, I, to reconstruct Whittier's phrases, found the "flinty slopes" too "hard" and the "new-mown sward" too "stubble-speared." As a result, putting on shoes for the first day of school each fall was not a problem.

In time I graduated to leather-soled shoes. The trouble with dust in the shoes persisted, but now there was another concern. Leather soles wore out, and we wore them long enough to wear them out. What to do? Like the saucy cobbler in the opening scene of Shakespeare's *Julius Caesar*—"A surgeon to old shoes" and "a mender of bad soles"—we operated on our shoes. The easiest way was to cut out a snug cardboard insole—we became adept at getting the right fit—and place it inside the shoe. This would be all right for Sunday wear, when we did not walk around much, but otherwise was just not serviceable. The cardboard covering the hole would wear through, again exposing sock (or foot).

Novelist George Eliot has one of her characters say: "Boots and shoes are the greatest trouble of my life. Everything else one can turn and turn about, and make old look like new; but there's no coaxing boots and shoes to be better than they are." We tried.

My mother's father had repaired shoes locally (in addition to his farming and other "jack-of-all" trades), and we children felt that we, too, could make permanent repairs. Dad had bought a stand and several lasts at an auction sale, and with those we set to work.

Now we were cutting out leather outer half-soles from whatever was available—we even tried rubber ones from old inner tubes—and nailed them to the existing worn soles. We certainly made our old shoes more wearable than they were, if not better in appearance. But when the uppers wore out, perhaps after the shoes had been handed down to a younger brother, there could be no more "coaxing" them for further use. They would finally have to be discarded.

A common expression advises us to cast all useless things aside just as we would an old shoe: that is, why hang on to old footwear? Another adage, in somewhat different tone, has it that the old shoes should not be flung just away, but also after their one-time wearer. It was good luck to do so, and a variation of the custom is still practiced today when shoes are being tied behind a departing wedding car.

But when I was a boy, we seemed loath to part with our shoes (unless they were beyond repair), whichever direction they might be flung. Partly, of course, this was because of necessity, and we prolonged their use so long as they enabled us to walk anywhere with our feet safe and sound. There was a comfort in old shoes, after all. Canadian poet Bliss Carman speaks of "an easy shoe" in "The Joys of the Road." And an old 1930s popular song simply starts with this line as an invitation to take a walk: "Put on an old pair of shoes."

So, in those good old days with our repaired shoes—runners, workboots, and once-fancy black shoes, ankle-high, laced, and double-toed—we were ready for the adventures of the day.

From Crayon to Casein

Having an uncle who painted, replete with palette and easel, was enough to stir any boy's interest in art, particularly in the hard-up days of the Depression when we all needed, in Robert Frost's phrase, to "get some … color out of life." My dad's brother, Uncle Jake, a bachelor and one-time teacher, had left his paying job to stroll about the countryside and pursue non-paying hobbies such as painting.

One fall in 1938, when he came by for a visit, he slipped off his packsack in our porch and did not slip it back on until several weeks later. He simply ensconced himself at our farm home—wanting some company, I suppose—and fell in with our everyday activities. At night he slept in the summer kitchen on an old door set upon two trestles. Near the end of his stay, he felt he should pay for his "board and room" and decided to do so with some artwork: a painting of our yard.

He stretched a piece of canvas over some stiff cardboard, set up his easel on the roof of our barn's lean-to, and opened his case of oil paints. His view was the mid-yard with its dominant woodpile and array of old farm machinery, the summer kitchen on one side and our "little gray home" at the end. The background was two large poplar bluffs, which sheltered the yard, and a lane leading to the horizon.

It was great adventure for me—I was but five years old—to

217

scramble up the ladder onto the lean-to and watch my uncle brush on the oils. He worked on his painting for days, it seemed, concentrating on the grasses and foliage. The trees were changing color as he painted, and he redid the bushes several times in order to capture their vivid autumnal tints. His was not a "genre" painting, for he left out the woodpile, machinery, and any of us who might be working in the yard (although he told me that if I walked into the summer kitchen and closed the door behind me, I, for one, would be *in* the painting).

Finished, the picture hung in our living room for years, a conversation piece for any guests, for few among them had a real painting in their house. (Free calendars, with a single illustration, were the usual pictures gracing Depression homes.) It intrigued them. As for me, art became an important part of my life.

In our one-room country school, I began my "career" as an artist—"Draw something!" was the teacher's frequent instruction to fill time. I should say immediately that I never had an easy knack for drawing things. Yet I believe I had a skill at "seeing" things, and then, by an effort of will, getting them down on paper.

One day, I remember, while I was still in grade one, our teacher printed the title BE KIND TO ANIMALS on the blackboard and asked us to copy it in our exercise books. Then he told us to draw a picture to illustrate the dictum. Although I had never seen a sheep, I chose to draw it as an animal to "be kind to"—I must have seen a photo of one. As I started to draw, I saw the sheep magically take shape on the page before me, perfect in proportion, sheeplike in every way. I enclosed it in a frame and added some green grass and blue sky.

Now it was my turn to be intrigued, and when the teacher was free to check our work, I guess he was, too. He held it up for the other grades to see, and during recess several of the older students came around to have a closer look. I was flattered, of course, but the main reason that I can recall the whole episode, I think, was that the drawing was not as broad as the title, and in trying to fit the picture to the words I had extended the grass and sky at one side (beyond the frame) and produced a patched-up picture.

My next artistic achievement was one I had to be cajoled into doing. A farm weekly we subscribed to was running a coloring contest for primary students. Coloring someone else's drawing was never what I wanted to do, decidedly so when it was a dainty rendition of a nursery rhyme. (I wanted to draw and color my own pictures—of cowboy country, for instance, or of woodsmen about an evening campfire.) However, my much older sister prevailed, filling out the entry form and supplying me with pencil crayons.

A conscientious child, I colored carefully, getting an even shade over broad areas and never once going past the lines. A few weeks later, in an envelope addressed to "Master Victor Friesen," a letter informed me that I had won first prize, to be sent under separate cover. The prize almost scuttled my interest in art then and there: it was a giant coloring book.

In grade four we had a new teacher, fresh out of normal school, with new ideas about teaching art, one of which involved trying "pastels" rather than the usual wax crayons. Pastels were like sticks of colored chalk but mixed with some base so that their color adhered well to paper. At the same time, with their complementary chalky nature, the colors, once applied, could be mixed with others, melded by fingertips or a piece of cloth. Although the colors were pale, the technique in using them was akin to painting with oils, without the fuss of using oil or cleaning fluids.

There was one problem. Although it was 1942, farmers had hardly come out of the Depression, and most parents could not afford to buy this frill for their children. What to do? The teacher asked if our parents could afford to buy *half* a box (there were about six crayons per box). We all checked at home and reported next day that it would be possible. So our teacher ordered but half a supply of pastels and cut each box, container and crayons, in half, crosswise. Then she closed the open-ended boxes by pasting on brown paper.

The whole classroom was elated with this new medium. We could barely wait for the next art period, and after that we stayed in at recesses to work on our pictures, walking about to see how our classmates were faring and discussing how someone had achieved a certain unique effect or blend of colors. We were like an artists' colony rather than a rural school, and the excitement lasted all of that winter.

In the senior elementary grades, watercolor became another medium. As farm incomes improved, we could all afford to buy a "paint box." It consisted of a long thin metal container with eight cakes of color, a partition for holding brushes, and a lid divided into three parts that, when opened, could be used for water and mixes. Now we were all watercolorists, learning how to apply even washes, trying always for a light and deft brush stroke. Again we compared results and discussed techniques.

A town cousin suggested that I enter a watercolor in the local fair or exhibition. Why not? By this time I had been experimenting with my paints, applying different colored washes to most objects in the painting, then using black separately to get the desired gradations to give textures and contours. I entered one such work and also a pencil drawing.

Meanwhile, another cousin and I, in emulation of our Uncle Jake, had begun to try out oils. We had each bought (that is, ordered from a catalog) a "student's" box of paints. The tubes were no bigger than a little finger. There is an engaging smell to oil paints, and we longed to use them at once, but first we had to find a suitable surface to paint on. The one thing in full supply was old oilcloth, once used to cover kitchen tables. When replaced, it was stored in rolls in the garage (nothing was ever thrown away). Oilcloth for oil paints seemed appropriate, although we used the reverse side, which had a cheesecloth backing.

On my birthday in midsummer, I wandered with paints and

oilcloth into the pasture. There, amid clumps of willow and trembling aspen, I tried to capture the pastoral scene—fluffy clouds, leafy trees, and bowed grasses. My mother thought I might be up to something like this and came out looking for me to see how I had progressed. She stood over me as I hunched cross-legged above my work and remarked: "You'll never forget this day." I have not either, not because of the painting I made—it has long been discarded—but because of the scene seen clearly, etched in my memory through the kinesthetic act of trying to paint it.

My father was also an appreciative onlooker of my artistic efforts in our pasture. On one occasion I was sketching a ground squirrel there, with pad and pencil, when he saw me. He hurried into the house and told Mother what I was doing. "Just like Jake," he said, beaming. Uncle Jake, I think, was his favorite brother.

At school, I had my own opportunity to appreciate the works of others, for the study of famous paintings was an important part of our grades seven and eight art. The prints we studied were invariably small, only about three by four-and-a-half inches, but we pored over them diligently, writing out descriptions under such headings as Center of Interest, Colors, Lines, Shapes, Design, and Other Features.

Our European paintings included Raphael's "Sistine Madonna," Rembrandt's "The Night Watch," Franz Hals's "The Laughing Cavalier," Hobbema's "Avenue of Trees," Vermeer's

"The Cook," Millet's "The Angelus," Rosa Bonheur's "The Horse Fair," Gainsborough's "The Blue Boy," and Turner's "The Fighting Téméraire." There were a few works of American and Canadian art, for example, by Winslow Homer and Tom Thomson. We studied the painters' lives as well. A teachers' journal carried these biographies, and we wrote out one-page summaries of each.

We were blessed with much bigger reproductions of paintings in current magazines. Each carried a full-color cover, with no superimposed obscuring headlines. Inside, painted illustrations, not photographs, were the chief accompaniments to stories and articles. Here was a world of art.

My appreciation and artistic endeavors carried over into my first two years of high school in the late 1940s, when I chose art as one of my elective subjects. As a result I did a variety of artwork—watercolors, India-ink sketches, pencil drawings, poster designs—and continued studying prints of famous paintings. Now the focus was on later artists such as the French Impressionists (Monet, Renoir) and the Canadian Group of Seven (A. Y. Jackson, J. E. H. MacDonald, F. H. Varley, and Arthur Lismer), also Cezanne and Van Gogh.

After high school, my interest in art received a boost when I attended normal school. There, Wynona Mulcaster was an inspiring art teacher, not only turning us into better teachers of art in the classroom but also prompting us to take further classes, at Emma Lake Art School. Through her I had three of my paintings shown in a traveling provincial exhibition that year, and four years later I took the pilgrimage to Emma Lake for a summer session.

The art instructors, Kenneth Lochhead and Arthur McKay (two of the Regina Group of Five), gave me a good grounding in drawing, teaching me to work in bits all over the page in order to achieve unity in composition; also to use thumb (or hand) to screen out parts of a work to see if every part indeed contributed to the whole.

The experience of living in an artists' colony continued to influence me long after the six-week program concluded. Some years later I contemplated spending a full two years at a regular art school and wrote away for its brochure, but that turned out to be a road not taken. Still, I began painting in casein, which the two instructors had been using in their own work. Casein, a versatile medium, comes in tubes like oil paint but is water-soluble. It can therefore be used thick, spread with a palette knife, or thinned, brushed on in a wash. I enjoyed working with it in either oil-paint or watercolor applications (or any variations in between) and painted still lifes set up in my light-housekeeping room and landscapes in the out-of-doors.

Art was a large part of my life for the next few years. When I was not painting (sometimes under an umbrella rigged up on a stand), I was pencil sketching anything that caught my eye—an orange-crate washstand in my room or a scenic ferry crossing. Before I painted anything, I sketched it a dozen times from various angles, just to get the feel of the subject. I subscribed to an art journal, read voluminous art histories, and regularly visited art galleries.

And then I came to a daunting realization: art could be an all-consuming passion; that it demanded, if one were to achieve real success, not just periods of intense discipline of the mind but an ongoing training of the whole body, the entire self (body and mind—and soul, too), a lifelong dedication of one's being. And I, like Henry David Thoreau on leaving Walden Pond after two years, knew that I had other interests to pursue—in writing, nature study, and music.

So my "career" as an artist came to a fairly abrupt end. I told myself that when I retired—say, at seventy-five—I might take up the brush again. I hope to. Meanwhile, I have taken up landscape photography, which is not so time-consuming. It answers my need to create visually, to capture, on film instead of canvas, the glorious colors and textures, the splendid lines and shapes, of that wild nature that ever haunts me with its incredible beauty.

Teaching at Stoney Lake

Wingard is one of Saskatchewan's oldest communities, having been first settled in 1882, three years before the resistance led by Louis Riel occurred in the surrounding area. Situated some six miles northeast of Fort Carlton, Wingard was never a regular town site. Rather, the name applied to a rural post office established in a farmer's home—that of Nels Peterson, a one-time ship's carpenter, gold miner, and fur trader who had come west by wagon train and named the place after a site in his native Denmark. Nearby, each at a separate location but all bearing the name "Wingard," were a ferry crossing (on the North Saskatchewan River), an Anglican log church, and a community hall. A school was there, too, and it and the area it served were registered as the Stoney Lake School District, No. 208. It was here that I began my teaching career. I taught there for two years, 1952 to 1954, with a starting annual salary of $1,800.

I can well remember first seeing the area when I signed my contract (I still have the original document). It was July 7, 1952, when I got into our Model A Ford and drove north past Carlton and on into the Wingard district. I was not yet nineteen, and there I was, seeking my fortune in the world, with all the ideals of the teaching profession still ringing in my ears from my previous year's attendance at normal school.

Opposite Wingard Hall, I had a brief glimpse of the school,

more or less surrounded by bushes, but my immediate destination was the home of Mr. Syd Peterson, grandson of Nels and secretary of the school board, so I continued two miles farther north. Along the way I passed the little, white, high-steepled church, glistening in the sunshine from its hilltop position, a landmark for miles around. Mr. Peterson and I returned at once to the school to look over the situation.

The first thing that we noticed on walking into the building was a gopher lying dead upon the floor. It must have come in through a cold-air duct, and Mr. Peterson apologized for not having a screen fastened in place. In fact, he assumed an apologetic manner for most of the things he explained about the school as he pointed out one failing after another. This struck me as an odd way of trying to interest a prospective teacher, particularly when there was a shortage of teachers and some of the neighboring schools had to make do with study supervisors. But it was his straightforward honesty in these matters that, more than anything, made me sign the contract that day.

When school started, it did not take long to fall into the new routine of classroom activity. The students were well meaning and cooperative so that my work as a beginning teacher went smoothly enough. The parents were just as friendly. I was boarding at the Peterson home, but before long various families were inviting me out to supper ("teacher for company"). What beaming faces greeted me around the lamplit tables—parents and children, including preschoolers and some no longer attending school. What good conversations we had.

With all this friendship and goodwill, I was emboldened to ask the school board—Mr. Peterson, Henry Reimer, and chairman Bill Bergen—whether a teacherage might be built on the school grounds. It was short notice if one were to be ready before winter set in, but the board thought it a good idea, too, for my "rent" would be janitor work in the school—sweeping floors and making fires each morning. To speed up matters, the board bought an old fourteen-by-twenty-foot structure, still covered with remnants of tarpaper, which once had been a house but in the last years served as somebody's granary. The inside was just a shell, but new boards and shavings soon fixed that up. My mother and I moved in on Remembrance Day.

It was a relatively mild winter the first year, but heating the teacherage was something of a problem. There were neither storm windows nor doors, the building was sitting directly on the ground without foundation, and the floor was but a single layer of warped boards. Anything left standing on the floor overnight (a pail of water, for instance) would be frozen the next morning. To get the maximum benefit out of the fuel wood, which had not seasoned fully, I stacked a portion of it behind the range, where daytime room temperatures would help to dry it out, and from this supply I would place a smaller portion for heating in the oven for more immediate use.

Doing so gave me another idea. Instead of putting on ice-cold shoes upon waking, why not slip them into the oven, too, and wear just my overshoes while walking to the school at 6:30 AM to get the fires there underway. Thereafter, I "baked" my shoes every morning before dressing for school. Nobody could say that I started my teaching day with cold feet!

The water supply was another concern. *Stoney* Lake was an apt name for the school—not only because of a lake nearby. Even the topsoil of the schoolyard was underlain with a bed of large stones, lying like eggs in a nest. It was almost impossible to dig a well by hand. But through the goodness of the Petersons, we were kept in supply, and I hauled water with a cream can when I could. To eke out this amount, we added prodigious quantities of clean snow to our pail of drinking water and snow not so clean to a barrel standing in the teacherage for other use. That way we had both "washing snow" and "drinking snow."

The following summer the people of the district did a lot of work on the teacherage, adding a foundation, a porch, plasterboard on the inside walls, and brick siding without. It was just as well, for the next January, 1954, was one of the coldest on record.

For many days the thermometer registered more than 50° below Fahrenheit, and I recall the weatherman on the radio saying that if the cold snap held out we would have the coldest January ever. A mild spell set in for the last three days, however, and continued all of the next month.

I had shoveled snow against our walls for insulation, higher than the window ledges, so we had a kind of snug harbor in the woods. It was nice to look out the west window in the evening at a winter sunset or to step outside on a bright moonlit night and see and hear a great horned owl, in rooster fashion, hooting from the school roof. Sometimes on going out the next day into the crisp morning air, I would find deer tracks encircling the little teacherage.

Other highlights at Stoney Lake were the Christmas concerts, highlights of any rural school year. Ours were held in the hall across the road and drew audiences from several districts. Plays enacting a classroom scene were popular, as was a play in which a "family" debated whether the best place to go for holidays was MacDowall or Leckford, two nearby communities. Star drills with colored crêpe paper and tinsel costumes kept everyone entertained, while the old barrel heater at the back of the hall glowed red from the huge lengths of wood fed into it.

I remember also the means by which the students came undaunted to school. One boy came by bicycle (a Christmas present) in the dead of winter, pedaling along a sleigh track. Others came by horse and cutter or caboose in winter and by buggy or sulky in summer, and one little girl in grade two sometimes rode a horse bareback. Most students walked, and during that very cold January one of the boys hiked some four miles each morning in order not to miss a single lesson.

Finally, I recall that a literature selection on the course of studies, fittingly, was an excerpt from David Grayson, *Adventures in Contentment*, a book about farm life. I shared the author's appreciation of rural activities, and my stay at Stoney Lake furnished many of the pleasures of country living.

When I left Wingard in June of 1954, electrification was just coming to the area. I was glad that I had been able to teach there, in a single-room school similar to the one I had attended and where life was much as it had been when I was a boy, with coal-oil lamps and wood-burning kitchen ranges. My experiences in my "first school" remain among my fondest memories, an adult extension of good old days on the farm that I would not experience throughout an entire year again.